S0-BMX-637

GRAMMAR
Form and Function 3

Workbook

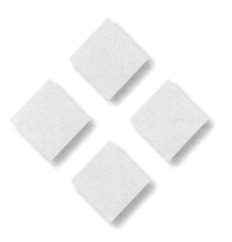

Milada Broukal
Diana Renn
Amy Parker

McGraw-Hill

Grammar Form and Function 3 Workbook

Published by McGraw-Hill ESL/ELT, a business unit of The McGraw-Hill Companies, Inc., 1221 Avenue of the Americas, New York, NY 10020. Copyright © 2005 by The McGraw-Hill Companies, Inc. All rights reserved. No part of this publication may be reproduced or distributed in any form or by any means, or stored in a database or retrieval system, without the prior written consent of The McGraw-Hill Companies, Inc., including, but not limited to, in any network or other electronic storage or transmission, or broadcast for distance learning.

 This book is printed on recycled, acid-free paper containing 10% postconsumer waste.

2 3 4 5 6 7 8 9 079/055 11 10 09 08 07 06 05

ISBN: 0-07-008314-2

Editorial director: Tina B. Carver
Executive editor: Erik Gundersen
Senior developmental editor: Annie Sullivan
Editorial assistant: Kasey Williamson
Production manager: MaryRose Malley
Cover design: Preface, Inc.
Interior design: Preface, Inc.

Photo credits:
All photos are courtesy of Getty Images Royalty-Free Collection.

Contents

UNIT 7   MODALS II

UNIT 8   THE PASSIVE VOICE, CAUSATIVES, AND PHRASAL VERBS

UNIT 9   GERUNDS AND INFINITIVES

UNIT 10   AGREEMENT AND PARALLEL STRUCTURE

UNIT 13   ADVERB CLAUSES

UNIT 14   CONDITIONAL SENTENCES

UNIT 1 THE PRESENT TENSES

1a The Simple Present Tense and The Present Progressive Tense

Student Book p. 2

☐1 Practice

Complete the sentences with the simple present or the present progressive of the verbs in parentheses. If there are other words in the parentheses, include them.

Jenna: Hi, Mark! I (never, see)

_____ you outside
                 1

this early in the morning. Where

(you, go) _____?
                              2

Mark: I (run) _____ to
                         3

the park right now. These days I

(try) _____ to work
                  4

out every morning before work. I (want) _____ to lose
                                                                     5

weight. My doctor said that exercise (be) _____ the most
                                                                6

important thing you can do. What about you? Why (be) _____
                                                                              7

you up so early?

Jenna: I (work out) _____ this morning, too. I usually
                                      8

(get up) _____ at six to work out.
                         9

Mark: That's great. What (you, do) _____ to stay in shape?
                                                      10

Jenna: Sometimes I (jog) _____ around the neighborhood. I often
                                          11

(take) _____ a yoga class at the gym. But unfortunately, it
                  12

(become) _____ more difficult to find the time and energy
                         13

to exercise.

Mark: Oh, really? Why (be) _____ it so hard?
                                              14

(be) _____ you busy with work?
                15

Jenna: Yes, I (be) _____ 16 . Sometimes I

(come) _____ 17 home late, and often I

(stay) _____ 18 up late finishing work. It

(get) _____ 19 harder to wake up early.

Mark: It (be) _____ 20 hard for me to get up in the morning and

exercise, too. But I (not, be) _____ 21 busy with work. I just

(not, like) _____ 22 to exercise!

2 Practice

Complete the questions and answers with the simple present or the present progressive of the verbs in parentheses. If there are other words in the parentheses, include them.

Doctor: How (you, feel) _____ 1 these days, Rob?

Rob: I (not, do) _____ 2 very well at the moment. I hurt my knee last Sunday, and the pain (get) _____ 3 worse. My knee (constantly, hurt) _____ 4 .

Doctor: (you, take) _____ 5 any medication right now?

Rob: No, I (not, take) _____ 6 anything at the moment.

Doctor: (you, exercise) _____ 7 regularly?

Rob: No, I don't. I (not, have, usually) _____ 8 time. Although I (play, sometimes) _____ 9 basketball with my friends on weekends.

Doctor: Which knee (bother) _____ 10 you?

Rob: My right knee.

Doctor: (it, hurt) _____ 11 when you bend your knee?

Rob: No, it (not, do) _____. But I (feel, always)
        _____ 12
        _____ pain when I straighten it.
        _____ 13

Doctor: How (your knee, feel) _____ when I move it this way?
        _____ 14

Rob: Ouch!

Doctor: You needed to see a doctor as soon as this happened. Who

        (be) _____ your regular doctor?
        _____ 15

Rob: I (see, usually) _____ Dr. Berman. But he
        _____ 16

        (be) _____ on vacation this week.
        _____ 17

3 Practice

Match the sentences with the uses of the simple present and the present progressive.

Simple Present Tense	Present Progressive Tense
a. permanent situation	d. action in progress
b. repeated action	e. changing situation
c. general truth	f. action in progress around the present

_____ 1. Susan works as a programmer at a computer company in Seattle.

_____ 2. Many people in the computer industry are losing their jobs these days.

_____ 3. There used to be many programming jobs in Seattle, but it is getting more difficult to find a job in today's economy.

_____ 4. Many companies advertise jobs in the newspaper.

_____ 5. Susan reads the job ads every morning.

_____ 6. A company called "Software Solutions" is hiring computer programmers right now!

4 Practice

Read the sentences. Write _C_ next to the sentence if the simple present or the present progressive is used correctly. Write _I_ if it is used incorrectly.

_____ **1.** Why you studying English at this school?

_____ **2.** Public transportation becomes more important in our crowded city.

_____ **3.** My sister is constantly borrowing my clothes.

_____ **4.** Because of her new diet, she's not eat bread now.

_____ **5.** These days, I'm working part time and going to school.

_____ **6.** Which movie you want to see?

_____ **7.** In the evenings, we like to walk around the neighborhood.

_____ **8.** Where do you working at present?

5 Practice

Look at the photo. Write four sentences using the simple present and four sentences using the present progressive. Try to include some negatives and questions.

Simple Present

1. _____

   _____

2. _____

   _____

3. _____

   _____

4. _____

Present Progressive

5. _____

6. _____

7. _____

8. _____

6 Practice

Complete the sentences with the simple present or the present progressive of the verbs in parentheses. If there are negative words in the parentheses, include them.

---

27 _____ **January 10, 2005**

Restaurant Review: The Boston Bistro

If you (look) _____ for 1

excellent food and a pleasant dining experience, do not

eat at the Boston Bistro. First of all, the food

(be) _____ terrible. The meat 2

(be) _____ tough and overcooked; it 3

(require) _____ a very sharp knife to cut it. 4

I (love) _____ garlic, but the pasta sauce 5

(smell) _____ too strongly of garlic. Strangely, 6

the sauce (not, taste) _____ like garlic — it (seem) _____ 7   8

to have no flavor at all! Finally, the menu (not, have) _____ many choices. 9

The food (not, be) _____ the only bad part of the Boston Bistro. The 10

dining room (appear) _____ crowded because there are so many tables 11

pushed together. Personally, I usually (not, enjoy) _____ the sound of loud 12

conversations around me while I (try) _____ to enjoy a quiet meal. Also, 13

the servers always (seem) _____ too busy to pay attention to you. 14

Above all, the food (cost) _____ too much. I (realize) 15

_____ many nice restaurants (charge) _____ more than 16   17

$25.00 for dinner these days. But for $28.00, I (prefer) _____ to have 18

excellent food and excellent service. I (fear) _____ that at those high 19

prices, the Boston Bistro won't be in business for long.

Decide if each sentence has a stative or an active meaning. Then complete the
sentences with the correct form of the verbs in parentheses.

1. (think)

He _____

about quitting his job.

However, he _____

_____ it

might be a bad idea.

2. (taste)

She _____ the ice

cream cone right now.

It _____ like

a coconut.

3. (smell)

The refrigerator

_____

terrible. She _____

_____

the refrigerator after

returning from her

vacation.

4. (appear)

The woman _____ very tired.

She _____ in a play

every night this week.

5. (be)

She _____ very quiet.

She _____ quiet because

she is working in a library.

The Present Perfect Tense and The Present Perfect Progressive Tense

Student Book p. 11

8 **Practice**

Complete the sentences with the present perfect or the present perfect progressive of the verbs in parentheses. Sometimes both tenses are possible. If both are possible, use the present perfect progressive.

A. Rachel, Eric, and Denise (graduate, just)

_____! They (attend)
1

_____ this school for
2

the past four years. All three of them

(wait) _____ a long time for this
3

special day. Rachel (study) _____
4

music, and she plans to continue her musical

studies in the future. Eric (find, already) _____ a good job in
5

a bank. Denise (decide) _____ to travel — she
6

(not, go) _____ anywhere since she started school. They
7

(not, say) _____ goodbye to all of their friends yet, and they
8

(still, not, remove) _____ their graduation caps and gowns.
9

They (be) _____ too busy celebrating their success.
10

B. Adina (try) _____ to
1
improve her grades in math for months. So far, her

grades (improve) _____.
2

Her teacher, Mr. Williams, (help)

_____ her. She
3

(study) _____ math for
4

two hours every night. She

(review) _____ all the
5

chapters in her math book. Adina (never, be)

_____ very good at math. She
6

(not, earn) _____ an "A" in math since she was in the ninth grade.
7

She (always, prefer) _____ English and foreign languages. But she
8

(just, receive) _____ an "A" on her math test.
9

9 | Practice

Circle the adverbs and time expressions. Then complete the sentences with the simple past, present perfect, or present perfect progressive of the verbs in parentheses. If either the present perfect or present perfect progressive is possible, use the present perfect progressive.

A. Robin: _____ (you, borrow) my new dress last night?
1

Joanna: No, I (not, do) _____. I (not, borrow)
2

_____ your clothes in a long time. Ever since I
3

gained a few pounds, I (not, be able to) _____
4

fit into your clothes.

Robin: That's strange. I (think) _____ I put the dress in my
5

closet right after I (come) _____ home yesterday.
6

B. Erica: I like your new car! When (you, buy) _____ it?

 David: I (buy) _____ it at 2:00 today. I (only, have) _____ it for a few hours!

 Erica: It's really bright. I (never, see) _____ you in such a colorful car. (you, own, ever) _____ a red car before?

 David: No, this is my first. I (always, prefer) _____ black cars. I (drive) _____ a black car since the day I (get) _____ my driver's license.

 Erica: So why (you, decide) _____ to buy a red car?

 David: This one (be) _____ on sale!

C. Samantha: (you, watch) _____ the baseball game last night?

 Ron: No, I (do, not) _____. I (never, like) _____ baseball.

 Samantha: You're kidding! Baseball (be) _____ this country's most popular sport for almost 100 years! Everybody likes baseball!

 Ron: Not me. I prefer soccer. I (be) _____ a soccer fan since I was a kid. And I (play) _____ the game for about ten years. (you, ever, see) _____ the World Cup on TV? Now that's exciting to watch.

 Samantha: I (watch) _____ the World Cup two years ago. You're right; it (be) _____ exciting to watch. I think Americans (grow) _____ more interested in soccer in recent years. But I still like baseball better.

10 Practice

Circle the correct adverb and put it in the correct position. Only one adverb is correct. Rewrite each sentence with the adverb in the correct place.

1. Gina has walked to work in her new shoes.
(still / just / ever)

_____

_____

2. She has worn such uncomfortable shoes.
(ever / yet / never)

_____

_____

3. It is only 9:00 in the morning, but her feet have started to hurt. (yet / still / already)

_____

_____

4. She hasn't arrived at work. (already / yet / just)

_____

11 Practice

Rewrite each sentence in Practice 10 as a question. Use the present perfect or present perfect progressive. Change adverbs if necessary.

1. _____ ?

2. _____ ?

3. _____ ?

4. _____ ?

12 Practice

Read the sentences. Write _C_ next to the sentence if the present perfect or the present perfect progressive is used correctly. Write _I_ if it is used incorrectly.

_____ **1.** She's been having that coat for a week.

_____ **2.** I so far have traveled to five countries and thirty states.

_____ **3.** The students have been waiting for the teacher since 20 minutes.

_____ **4.** Have they already paid for their tickets?

_____ **5.** Where has the time gone?

_____ **6.** Have ever you been to Africa?

_____ **7.** He hasn't returned the homework already.

_____ **8.** Women have been earned more money for the last ten years.

_____ **9.** How many times have you been taking the TOEFL?

_____ **10.** We've never been to that restaurant.

13 Practice

Write five statements and two questions about the people in the photo. Use the tenses given in parentheses and time expressions, adverbs, or negatives when possible.

1. (present perfect)

_____

2. (present perfect progressive)

_____

3. (simple past)

_____

4. (simple present)

_____

5. (present progressive)

_____

6. (Question: present perfect)

_____

7. (Question: present perfect progressive)

_____

SELF-TEST

A **Choose the best answer, A, B, C, or D, to complete the sentence. Mark your answer by darkening the oval with the same letter.**

1. Who _____ to join us for lunch?

   A. does want   Ⓐ Ⓑ Ⓒ Ⓓ
   B. is wanting
   C. wants
   D. wanting

2. Many students _____ at part-time jobs these days.

   A. have worked   Ⓐ Ⓑ Ⓒ Ⓓ
   B. are working
   C. working
   D. are being working

3. Basketball players _____ usually tall.

   A. are being   Ⓐ Ⓑ Ⓒ Ⓓ
   B. are
   C. have been
   D. being

4. What grade _____ in that class?

   A. are you having   Ⓐ Ⓑ Ⓒ Ⓓ
   B. you have
   C. have
   D. do you have

5. Fresh coffee _____ good in the morning.

   A. is smelling   Ⓐ Ⓑ Ⓒ Ⓓ
   B. has been smelling
   C. smells
   D. smelling

6. Anne: Are you enjoying that book?
   Ron: Yes, _____.

   A. I'm   Ⓐ Ⓑ Ⓒ Ⓓ
   B. I have
   C. I am
   D. I do

7. Right now, she _____ about her vacation.

   A. thinks   Ⓐ Ⓑ Ⓒ Ⓓ
   B. has thought
   C. has been thinking
   D. is thinking

8. The class _____ $100 for their trip.

   A. earns   Ⓐ Ⓑ Ⓒ Ⓓ
   B. has earned
   C. has been earning
   D. earning

9. She _____ to borrow her parents' car.

   A. is constantly asking   Ⓐ Ⓑ Ⓒ Ⓓ
   B. constantly asking
   C. asking constantly
   D. is constantly asks

10. Why _____ TV for four hours?

    A. they have watched   Ⓐ Ⓑ Ⓒ Ⓓ
    B. have they watched
    C. have they been watching
    D. they are watching

B Find the underlined word or phrase, A, B, C, or D, that is incorrect. Mark your answer by darkening the oval with the same letter.

1. He <u>hasn't</u> <u>answered</u> <u>so far</u> our question
        A   B   C

   <u>about the test</u>.
       D

   Ⓐ Ⓑ Ⓒ Ⓓ

2. Mary <u>hasn't</u> <u>been</u> <u>work</u> <u>at her new job</u> for
          A   B   C   D

   very long.

   Ⓐ Ⓑ Ⓒ Ⓓ

3. <u>Where</u> <u>the baseball team has</u> <u>been</u>
     A   B   C

   <u>practicing</u> during the winter?
     D

   Ⓐ Ⓑ Ⓒ Ⓓ

4. <u>Have you</u> <u>yet</u> <u>signed up</u> for <u>the class</u>?
     A   B   C   D

   Ⓐ Ⓑ Ⓒ Ⓓ

5. <u>Her</u> mother <u>has been</u> <u>waiting</u> for her
     A   B   C

   <u>for 3:00</u> in the afternoon.
     D

   Ⓐ Ⓑ Ⓒ Ⓓ

6. The workers <u>are</u> <u>painting</u> the fence <u>since</u>
             A   B   C

   early <u>this morning</u>.
        D

   Ⓐ Ⓑ Ⓒ Ⓓ

7. I <u>haven't</u> <u>been</u> <u>still</u> to <u>any countries</u> in
      A   B   C   D

   Asia.

   Ⓐ Ⓑ Ⓒ Ⓓ

8. What is the most <u>exciting</u> thing you <u>have</u>
                 A   B

   <u>ever</u> <u>do</u>?
     C   D

   Ⓐ Ⓑ Ⓒ Ⓓ

9. <u>Is</u> the president <u>appears</u> on <u>any TV shows</u>
    A   B   C

   <u>this week</u>?
     D

   Ⓐ Ⓑ Ⓒ Ⓓ

10. <u>Some</u> older people <u>are believing</u> that
      A   B

    teenagers <u>are becoming</u> more <u>polite</u>
            C   D

    these days.

    Ⓐ Ⓑ Ⓒ Ⓓ

UNIT 2 THE PAST TENSES

2a   The Simple Past Tense and The Past Progressive Tense

Student Book p. 28

1   Practice

Complete the sentences with the simple past or the past progressive of the verbs in parentheses. If there are other words in the parentheses, include them.

Police Beat: A List of Last Week's Neighborhood Crimes

A.   On Saturday, April 12, a 70-year-old woman (report) _____ that her purse
                                                                    1
was stolen at Bradshaw's Supermarket. She (wait) _____ in the checkout line
                                                         2
when she suddenly (realize) _____ she needed to buy milk. When she (leave)
                                 3
_____ her grocery cart to get the milk, she (forget) _____ to
       4   5
take her purse with her. When she (return) _____ to the cart, her purse
                                                  6
(be) _____ gone. There (be) _____ two other people in line,
         7   8
two men in their 30s. The woman (ask) _____ them about her purse. They
                                            9
(not, see) _____ anything happen while they (stand) _____ in line.
               10   11
They (say) _____ that maybe she had left her purse somewhere else.
               12

B.   At 7:00 P.M. on Thursday, April 10, a man on Maple Street (water) _____
                                                                               1
his yard when he (hear) _____ a woman screaming. He immediately
                             2
(call) _____ the police on his cell phone. Then he (drop) _____ the
           3   4
hose and (run) _____ in the direction of the screams. At the end of the block,
                     5
he (see) _____ a tall man in a blue jacket trying to take the woman's briefcase.
             6
When the tall man (notice) _____ the neighbor, he (stop) _____
                                 7   8
what he (do) _____, (let) _____ go of the briefcase, and (turn)
                   9   10
_____ to leave. At first he (not, seem) _____ worried about the
       11   12
neighbor, but then he suddenly (start) _____ to run. The neighbor
                                             13
(not, want) _____ the man to escape before the police (come)
                 14
_____. He (yell) _____ at the tall man to stop. While the man
       15   16

(escape) _____ , he (trip) _____ over his shoelace and (fall)
      17   18

_____ to the ground. Seconds later, while he (try) _____ to stand
  19   20

up, police (arrive) _____ on the scene and (arrest) _____ the man.
          21   22

2 | Practice

Complete the sentences with the simple past or the past progressive of the verbs in parentheses. If there are other words in the parentheses, include them.

Mike Willis's life has always included bicycles.

Even as a very small child, he (love) _____
                                 1

bicycles. His parents (give) _____ him a
                        2

bike when he (be) _____ only four years
                  3

old. In high school, he (compete) _____
                         4

in many races, and he (win) _____ a lot
                  5

of money.

One day, while he (train) _____ for
                         6

a big race, he (feel) _____ a sharp pain in his chest. He (ignore)
                7

_____ it and kept riding. But as days (pass) _____ , the pain
  8   9

(not, go) _____ away. And it (get) _____ harder for him to ride
           10   11

his bike up hills or long distances.

Mike's parents (be) _____ very worried about their son. They (think)
                  12

_____ he had a virus. They (take) _____ him to the doctor. The
  13   14

doctor (do) _____ many tests on Mike's blood.
           15

The next day, while Mike (fix) _____ the gears on his bicycle, the doctor
                            16

(call) _____ . He (ask) _____ Mike to come to his office. There,
      17   18

the doctor (say) _____ that he (have) _____ a rare and very
           19   20

dangerous form of cancer. That same day, Mike (decide) _____ to do all he
                                      21

could to fight this disease. And he (promise) _____ himself that if he (get)
                                22

_____ well, he would help other people with cancer.
  23

15

Mike (keep) _____ his promise. Six months after he (recover)
                24

_____ from cancer, he (begin) _____ riding his bike. Eight
        25   26

months later, he (go) _____ on long rides again. In 2001, he (start)
                            27

_____ an annual bike riding event to raise money for cancer research. Three
        28

years later, more than 500 cyclists (participate) _____ in this event. In
                                                        29

2004, the event (raise) _____ nearly one million dollars for cancer research.
                              30

3 | Practice

Use the prompts to write yes/no questions and answers about Mike Willis. Use the simple past or the past progressive.

1. Mike / love / bicycles / as a child

Question: _____?

Answer: _____.

2. he / win / a lot of money / from bicycle races

Question: _____?

Answer: _____.

3. Mike / see / a doctor / as soon as he felt pain

Question: _____?

Answer: _____.

4. Mike's parents / worried / about him

Question: _____?

Answer: _____.

5. Mike / ride / his bike / while he was sick

Question: _____?

Answer: _____.

6. Mike / ride / his bike / by 2001

Question: _____?

Answer: _____.

4 Practice

Use the question words to write questions about Mike Willis for the answers that follow.

1. Question: When _____?

   Answer: Mike's parents gave him a bicycle when he was four years old.

2. Question: When _____?

   Answer: He first felt a pain in his chest while he was training for a big race.

3. Question: What _____?

   Answer: They thought he had a virus.

4. Question: What _____?

   Answer: Mike was fixing the gears on his bike when the doctor called.

5. Question: How soon after his recovery _____?

   Answer: Mike was going on long bike rides eight months after his recovery.

6. Question: How much _____?

   Answer: Mike's event raised nearly one million dollars in 2004.

7. Question: Why _____?

   Answer: Mike started this event because he promised to help people fight cancer.

5 Practice

Read the sentences. What does each sentence mean? Circle *a* or *b*.

1. My sister was very happy when she learned she got the job.

   a. First she was happy, and then she learned she got the job.

   b. She learned she got the job, and then she was very happy.

2. My sister was wondering if she should go back to school when she learned she got the job.

   a. First she was wondering if she should go back to school, and then she learned she got the job.

   b. She learned she got the job, and then she wondered if she should go back to school.

3. Our parents cried when they heard the good news.

   a. First our parents heard the good news, and then they cried.

   b. Our parents were crying, and then they heard the good news.

4. While Jack was traveling in Europe, his dog died.

    a. First Jack's dog died, and then Jack traveled in Europe.

    b. Jack went to Europe, and then his dog died.

5. Rosa called her sister when she heard that the baby was born.

    a. First Rosa heard that the baby was born, and then she called her sister.

    b. Rosa called her sister, and then the baby was born.

6. Tom's girlfriend came over while he was taking a nap.

    a. First Tom started to take a nap, and then his girlfriend came over.

    b. Tom's girlfriend came over, and then Tom took a nap.

6   Practice

Combine the sentences into one using *while* or *when*. Use correct punctuation.

1. I studied for the final exam. I didn't want to hear the TV or the phone.

    While _____.

2. I worked at two jobs. I never had any free time.

    _____ while _____.

3. My friends were upset. They heard we were moving to another city.

    When _____.

4. Elizabeth turned 16. More than 100 guests came to her birthday party.

    _____ when _____.

5. Josh applied to colleges. His parents hoped he would stay close to home.

    While _____.

7   Practice

Rewrite the sentences in Practice 6 with the *when* and *while* clauses in reverse order. Use correct punctuation.

1. _____.

2. _____.

3. _____.

4. _____.

5. _____.

8 | Practice

Complete the sentences with information about you, your friends, or your family.

1. _____ felt really embarrassed when _____

_____.

2. _____ was very afraid when _____

_____.

3. When _____,

_____ was very sad.

4. When _____,

_____ was extremely happy.

9 | Practice

Choose one of the sentences you wrote in Practice 8. Use it as the first sentence of a paragraph. In at least six sentences, give more information about what happened. Use the simple past and the past progressive tenses as you tell the story.

_____

_____

_____

_____

_____

_____

_____

_____

_____

_____

2b The Past Perfect Tense and The Past Perfect Progressive Tense

Student Book p. 36

10 Practice

Complete the sentences with the simple past or the past perfect of the verbs in parentheses. If there are other words in the parentheses, include them.

Have you ever won any money? My friend

Jason (feel) _____ like he did
                          1

yesterday. After work, he

(go) _____ to the bank to get
                2

some money. He (want) _____
                                    3

to take his girlfriend Lisa out to dinner at a

nice restaurant. They (not, eat)

_____ at a nice restaurant for weeks. Since he (just, be) _____
              4   5

paid at work, he (think) _____ it would be fun to spend a little more
                                    6

money.

At the cash machine, he (ask) _____ for $100.00. He
                                                    7

(be) _____ very surprised when a large number of $20.00 bills
                8

(start) _____ flying out! He (never, see) _____
                9   10

so much cash at one time. He (be) _____ alone at the machine,
                                                      11

and he (not, know) _____ what to do. He (wonder) _____
                              12   13

if this (happen, ever) _____ to anyone else.
                              14

Finally, the money (stop) _____ coming out. Jason
                                        15

(take) _____ the $20 bills from the ground and
              16

(count) _____ them. He (could not, believe) _____
              17   18

his luck. Just a few minutes earlier, he (think) _____ about taking his
                                                              19

girlfriend somewhere nice. Now he could take her to the nicest place in town!

He (put) _____ the money in his wallet. He
                    20
(walk) _____ away from the machine. Then he
              21
(wonder) _____ if he (do) _____ the right thing.
                22   23
Maybe the machine (be) _____ broken. If so, the money
                            24
(not, be) _____ his to keep. Jason (bring) _____
              25   26
the money into the bank and (tell) _____ the manager what
                                        27
(happen) _____ to him at the cash machine. The manager said
              28
she (never, hear) _____ of that happening before. She
                        29
(be) _____ very glad that Jason (return) _____
        30   31
the money.

Jason (take) _____ Lisa out to dinner later that night, for less
                  32
than $100. Lisa (be) _____ happy. She (say) _____
                        33   34
it was the nicest evening she (enjoy) _____ in a long time. Then she
                                          35
said that Jason (spend) _____ too much money.
                              36

II Practice

Someone took this photo of Alyssa yesterday. Why did she look so happy? Complete the sentences using the prompts and the past perfect or the past perfect progressive.

1. (get a new job)

   She looked happy because

   _____.

2. (buy some new clothes)

   She looked happy because

   _____.

3. (work out during her lunch hour)

   She looked happy because _____.

4. (not / listen to the bad news on TV)

She looked happy because _____.

5. *(your idea)*

She looked happy because _____.

6. *(your idea)*

She looked happy because _____.

12 Practice

A journalist is interviewing an actor about his new movie. Use the prompts to write questions for the actor's answers. Write the questions in the simple past, the past perfect, or the past perfect progressive.

1. Question: When _____?

    Answer: I made this movie last summer.

2. Question: _____?

    Answer: No, I had never been in an action movie before.

3. Question: What kinds of movies _____?

    Answer: I had acted in romances and comedies.

4. Question: Why _____?

    Answer: I'd never done action movies because I wasn't in very good shape.

5. Question: Where _____?

    Answer: They filmed this movie in Turkey and in France.

6. Question: _____?

    Answer: No, I hadn't visited either of those countries before.

7. Question: What _____?

    Answer: Before I made this movie, I'd been taking a break from acting.

8. Question: Where _____?

    Answer: I'd been living in Los Angeles before I moved to New York.

9. Question: How long _____?

Answer: I'd been working in L.A. for about five years.

10. Question: How many _____?

Answer: I'd starred in eight movies.

13 Practice

Write six sentences about what you had or hadn't done (or been doing) by the time you sat down to do this exercise. Write three sentences using the past perfect and three sentences using the past perfect progressive. Use some negatives.

1. _____.

2. _____.

3. _____.

4. _____.

5. _____.

6. _____.

14 Practice

Complete the sentences with the present perfect progressive or the past perfect progressive of the verbs in parentheses.

1. The Larsen family is moving today. They (pack) _____ boxes since 6:00 in the morning.

2. Yesterday, they (pack) _____ for ten hours before they finally went to bed.

3. They're excited because they (want) _____ a bigger home for years.

4. Before they found this new home, they (complain) _____ that their apartment was too small for three people and two dogs.

5. They (move) _____ the furniture around, but it hadn't worked.

6. The Larsens were happy to find this new house because they (look) _____ for a long time.

Used To + Base Verb and *Would* + Base Verb

Student Book p. 44

15 **Practice**

Underline the correct forms in parentheses.

A.

1. When my grandparents were young, many people (had smoked / used to smoke) in public places.

2. Where (did people use to / people would) smoke?

3. People (would smoke / use to smoke) in almost any public place, including restaurants and movie theaters.

4. They (wouldn't think / didn't use to think) that smoking was dangerous.

5. My grandfather (would start / started) smoking back in college.

6. At that time, students and professors (had / would have) very different attitudes about cigarettes.

7. Some students (used to light / were used to light) cigarettes in the classroom!

B.

1. Romance today is different from in the past. In the 1940s, a man (used to "court" / was used to "court") a woman.

2. A true gentleman (would used to bring / would bring) a woman flowers every time he came to see her.

3. A woman (would try / used to trying) to win his love with clever conversation and charm, not just with appearance.

4. My grandmother (won / used to win) my grandfather's heart this way in 1941.

5. In that same year, he (used to ask / asked) her to marry him.

C.

1. In the past, people (used to dress / used to dressing) more formally than they do now.

2. In the 1940s, my grandmother (used to wear / wore) a skirt to work every day.

3. She also (wouldn't leave / didn't leave) her house without a matching hat and purse.

4. She (wouldn't wear / didn't wear) flat shoes with skirts.

5. She (used to walk / walked) everywhere in heels.

6. My grandfather (used to go / went) to work in a suit every day.

7. He (would work / worked) in the office from 8:00 till 6:00 five days a week.

8. Until the 1960s, most people (didn't use to go / use to not go) outside without a hat.

16 Practice

Look at the chart about the business world in the 1930s and the business world today. Write sentences about the 1930s with *used to* or *would* (or *didn't use to* / *wouldn't*) compared with today. Use the verbs in the chart.

	Businesspeople in the Past	Businesspeople Today
1.	type or write by hand	write on computers
2.	work only in the office	work from anywhere (like home)
3.	don't have good phone service	talk on cell phones with improved technology
4.	do a lot of business in person	don't always meet the people they do business with
5.	write letters	send and receive email
6.	don't dress informally	often wear informal clothes

1. _____ ,

   but now _____ .

2. Today, _____ ,

   but in the past, _____ .

3. _____ ,

   but these days _____ .

4. Now, _____ ;

   in contrast, in the past, _____ .

5. _____ ;

   however, today _____ .

6. These days, _____ ,

   whereas in the past, _____ .

|17| Practice

Do you see any changes from the recent past until now? Think about the 1980s or the 1990s. What did you use to do then that you don't do now? What would other people do? Write eight sentences with *used to* and *would*. Use the following verbs and your own ideas.

1. listen to / dance to

_____.

2. pay

_____.

3. go

_____.

4. like

_____.

5. wear

_____.

6. think

_____.

7. *your idea*

_____.

8. *your idea*

_____.

9. *your idea*

_____.

10. *your idea*

_____.

SELF-TEST

A **Choose the best answer, A, B, C, or D, to complete the sentence. Mark your answer by darkening the oval with the same letter.**

1. Maria failed the test. She _____ for it.

   A. didn't use to study   Ⓐ Ⓑ Ⓒ Ⓓ
   B. wasn't studying
   C. hadn't studied
   D. wasn't used to studying

2. While the children _____, the parents relaxed.

   A. had played   Ⓐ Ⓑ Ⓒ Ⓓ
   B. were playing
   C. used to play
   D. would play

3. Amy _____ at a restaurant, but now she works in an office.

   A. was used to working   Ⓐ Ⓑ Ⓒ Ⓓ
   B. use to work
   C. would work
   D. used to work

4. How many miles _____ in that old car?

   A. had he driven   Ⓐ Ⓑ Ⓒ Ⓓ
   B. he drove
   C. had he been driving
   D. he was driving

5. By the time the airplane landed, the passengers _____ for ten hours.

   A. flew   Ⓐ Ⓑ Ⓒ Ⓓ
   B. had been flying
   C. were flying
   D. would fly

6. What TV show _____ last night?

   A. have they watched   Ⓐ Ⓑ Ⓒ Ⓓ
   B. did they watch
   C. had they watched
   D. they were watching

7. The mother did everything she could, but her baby _____ crying.

   A. wouldn't stop   Ⓐ Ⓑ Ⓒ Ⓓ
   B. didn't use to stop
   C. hadn't stopped
   D. wasn't stopping

8. The family was eating breakfast when somebody _____ at the door.

   A. was knocking   Ⓐ Ⓑ Ⓒ Ⓓ
   B. had been knocking
   C. knocked
   D. had knocked

9. How long _____ by the time I got home?

   A. were you waiting   Ⓐ Ⓑ Ⓒ Ⓓ
   B. did you wait
   C. did you use to wait
   D. had you been waiting

10. Tim: Were you talking to me?
    John: No, I _____. I was talking to Bob.

    A. didn't   Ⓐ Ⓑ Ⓒ Ⓓ
    B. wasn't
    C. hadn't
    D. wouldn't

B **Find the underlined word or phrase, A, B, C, or D, that is incorrect. Mark your answer by darkening the oval with the same letter.**

1. I <u>drink</u> coffee <u>these days</u>, but I <u>didn't</u>
       A   B   C

   <u>used to</u>.
    D

   Ⓐ Ⓑ Ⓒ Ⓓ

2. <u>While</u> the woman <u>had been</u> <u>leaving</u> her
    A   B   C

   house, the telephone <u>rang</u>.
                     D

   Ⓐ Ⓑ Ⓒ Ⓓ

3. Before she <u>became</u> a dentist, Lisa <u>had</u>
            A   B

   <u>been</u> <u>being</u> an ice skater.
    C   D

   Ⓐ Ⓑ Ⓒ Ⓓ

4. He <u>had</u> <u>been running</u> twelve miles <u>when</u>
       A   B   C

   he suddenly <u>collapsed</u>.
             D

   Ⓐ Ⓑ Ⓒ Ⓓ

5. By the time we <u>were arriving</u>, the train
                A

   <u>had</u> <u>already</u> <u>left</u> the station.
    B   C   D

   Ⓐ Ⓑ Ⓒ Ⓓ

6. He <u>looked</u> healthy <u>because</u> he
       A   B

   <u>had been exercise</u> <u>regularly</u>.
         C   D

   Ⓐ Ⓑ Ⓒ Ⓓ

7. <u>Why</u> <u>hasn't</u> anyone <u>told us</u> that we <u>needed</u>
    A   B   C   D

   to be there by 3:00?

   Ⓐ Ⓑ Ⓒ Ⓓ

8. The soccer team <u>used to practice</u> six days
                 A

   <u>a week</u> in 1999, <u>but</u> they <u>aren't</u> now.
    B   C   D

   Ⓐ Ⓑ Ⓒ Ⓓ

9. <u>From the moment</u> the race <u>was starting</u>,
           A   B

   the black horse <u>led</u> all <u>the others</u>.
                C   D

   Ⓐ Ⓑ Ⓒ Ⓓ

10. Her grandparents <u>were</u> <u>used to</u> <u>live</u>
                 A   B   C

    in a house, but now they <u>live</u> in an
                           D

    apartment.

    Ⓐ Ⓑ Ⓒ Ⓓ

UNIT 3 THE FUTURE TENSES

3a *Be Going To* and *Will*

Student Book p. 58

1 Practice

Complete the sentences with the *be going to* or the *will* form of the verbs in parentheses.

A.

Todd: Oh no! I'm sorry. My dog has just eaten the cookies you baked!

Jennifer: Don't worry. I (bake)

     I'll bake some more.
         ₁
Do you think your dog

(get) _____ sick
             ₂
from eating all those cookies?

Todd: No, he _____. He (eat) _____ everything.
           ₃   ₄
But I think I (take) _____ him outside for a walk. He
                      ₅
(not, find) _____ anything interesting to eat out there.
                ₆

Jennifer: I'm afraid your dog (not, be) _____ very happy outside. It's
                            ₇
really cold. I think it (snow) _____.
                          ₈

Todd: I'm sure he (be) _____ fine. He has a lot of fur. That (keep)
                ₉
_____ him warm.
        ₁₀

B.

Kathy: (you, add) _____ more fruit to the smoothie?
1

I'm afraid the blender

(break) _____ .
2

There is already a lot of fruit in there.

Rick: The blender (not, break)

_____ .
3

Don't forget, I (be)

_____ a famous chef someday! I know what I'm doing.
4

Kathy: Yes, but the juice is already at the top of the blender.

It (spill) _____ .
5

Rick: I've been making this recipe for years. I've never had a problem with it before,

and I (not, have) _____ a problem with it now.
6

Kathy: There (be) _____ a big mess in the kitchen. I'm sure of it.
7

Rick: Then I (clean) _____ it up for you. Now, I (put)
8

_____ the lid on. Then I
9

(turn on) _____ the blender. Are you ready? Stand back!
10

2 Practice

A. Read the information from a brochure about yoga classes. Complete the sentences with *be going to* or *will* and verbs from the list.

be	meet
feel	offer
give	see
help	show
learn	teach
make	

Welcome to Yoga Journeys!

On February 6, Yoga Journeys _is going to offer_ a free class for
1
beginning yoga students. The class _____ from 1:00 to
2
2:30 at the main studio on Linden Avenue. Our master teacher, Donna Bliss,

_____ this class.
3

In this class, you _____ the basics of yoga positions.
4
With her gentle and supportive teaching style, Donna also _____
5
you how to breathe correctly. Because this is an introductory class, she

(not) _____ you do any complicated movements. Don't worry!
6

Over time, yoga practice _____ you strength and flexibility.
7
In one class, you probably (not) _____ instant results. But
8
you _____ more relaxed after just a few minutes of yoga.
9
Yoga _____ you to concentrate and to focus.
10
Our society is becoming more stressful, so yoga _____
11
an increasingly important way to manage stress in the future. Take a break

from stress. Come join us on a yoga journey!

B. Use the prompts to write yes/no and wh- questions. Use the *be going to* or the *will* form of the verb. Then use information from the reading in Part A to write answers.

1. when / Yoga Journeys / offer / a free class

   Question: _When is Yoga Journeys going to offer a free class?_

   Answer: _Yoga Journeys is going to (OR will) offer a free class on_
   February 6, from 1:00-2:30.

2. where / the class / meet

   Question: _____?

   Answer: _____.

3. who / teach / the class

   Question: _____?

   Answer: _____.

4. what / you / learn / in this class

   Question: _____?

   Answer: _____.

5. the teacher / make you learn / any complicated movements

   Question: _____?

   Answer: _____.

6. a yoga class / make / you / stronger and more flexible

   Question: _____?

   Answer: _____.

7. you / feel / strong and flexible / after just one class

   Question: _____?

   Answer: _____.

8. how / you / feel / after just a few minutes of yoga

   Question: _____?

   Answer: _____.

9. why / yoga / be / an increasingly important way to manage stress

   Question: _____?

   Answer: _____.

3 Practice

Think of a sport, hobby, or activity that you enjoy. Imagine you are going to offer a free class on this activity. Write six sentences using *be going to* + verb or *will* + verb. Then use the sentences to create a brochure like the one in Practice 2.

1. _____

2. _____

3. _____

4. _____

5. _____

6. _____

3b Time Clauses and Conditional Sentences in the Future

Student Book p. 63

4 Practice

Marco is traveling in Italy. Match the information in column A with the information in column B to make complete sentences from his letter home.

Dear Mom and Dad,

A

___i___ **1.** I can't believe it! When this train stops,

_____ **2.** While I'm traveling to Rome,

_____ **3.** I'm going to leave my backpack at the hotel

_____ **4.** After I check in to my hotel,

_____ **5.** I won't leave Rome

_____ **6.** I'll think of you both

_____ **7.** I'll buy nice gifts for everyone

_____ **8.** Unless I save some money,

_____ **9.** I'm going to take the train to Naples

_____ **10.** I'll write to you again

B

a. until I see the Trevi Fountain.

b. if I have enough money.

c. as soon as I get to Naples.

d. after I spend three days in Rome.

e. I won't be able to afford a ticket to Naples.

f. I'm going to visit the Coliseum.

g. before I go sightseeing in Rome.

h. while I'm eating gelato on the Spanish Steps.

i. I'll be in Rome!

j. I'll write to you about my plans.

5 Practice

Marco's parents are talking about his letter from Italy. Use the prompts to write their questions about Marco's travel plans. Write each question two ways: once with the time or condition clause at the beginning and once with it at the end. Use correct punctuation.

1. What / do / when / arrive / in Rome

   <u>What is Marco going to do when he arrives in Rome?</u>

   <u>When Marco arrives in Rome, what is he going to do?</u>

2. Where / go / after / leave / Rome

   _____

   _____

3. When / write / to us / after / visit / Naples

   _____

   _____

4. What / do / if / spend / all his money

   _____

   _____

5. How / ask for help / if / get lost

   _____

   _____

6. If / become sick / who / call

   _____

   _____

6 Practice

What are your plans for the future? Complete the sentences with a time clause, a condition clause, or a main clause.

1. As soon as I finish school, _____

   _____.

2. If I have enough money, _____

   _____.

3. I won't get a job _____

   _____.

4. Until I improve my English, _____

   _____.

5. Once I get a job, _____

   _____.

6. While I'm living here, _____

   _____.

7. After I've been living here a while, _____

   _____.

8. I'll be very happy _____

   _____.

9. I'll feel sad _____

   _____.

10. Before _____,

    _____.

11. _____ if

    _____.

12. When _____,

    _____.

3c Present Tenses with Future Meaning

Student Book p. 67

7 Practice

Complete the sentences with the present progressive or the simple present.

Amy: When (the store, open)

          does the store open ?
                 1

Salesclerk: We (open) _____
                      2

at 10:00 every day. Can you come

back?

Amy: I can't. It's 9:15 now, and I (start)

_____ work at 9:30.
            3

Salesclerk: This evening we (stay) _____

_____ open until
       4

7:30 because of the big shoe sale we

(have) _____. Can you come back later today?
          5

Amy: No. Today I (leave) _____ town right after work.
                     6

Salesclerk: The sale (continue) _____ all through the weekend.
                    7

You could return on Saturday or Sunday.

Amy: Actually, I (go) _____ out of town for the whole
                  8

weekend.

Salesclerk: I see. What day (come, you) _____ back?
                  9

Amy: I (return) _____ on Monday. But I've just remembered —
            10

I (not, work) _____ that day.
              11

(you, still, sell) _____ shoes at 40% off next week?
                 12

Salesclerk: No, we (not, be) _____. The sale
               13

(end) _____ on Monday.
       14

Practice

Keiko and Michael are making plans. Use the information to write sentences about their scheduled activities and arrangements. Use the simple present or the present progressive. The time clause may be at the beginning or the end of the sentence.

Around 6:30:	Michael picks Keiko up at home.
At 7:00:	Eat dinner at the Boston Bistro.
At 8:15:	Movie starts.
At 10:00:	Movie ends.
Around 10:15:	Go out for coffee and dessert.
After coffee and dessert:	Drive to a friend's party.
No later than 11:30:	Michael drives Keiko home.
At 8:00 A.M. the next day:	Keiko works.

1. _____ *Michael is picking Keiko up at home around 6:30.* _____

2. _____

3. _____

4. _____

5. _____

6. _____

7. _____

8. _____

3d The Future Progressive Tense

Student Book p. 70

9 **Practice**

Woodland College is having an open house for new students tomorrow. Use the schedule and prompts to write questions and answers about what will be happening at the open house. Use the future progressive tense.

Woodland College Open House Agenda

8:00 Students and parents arrive at the college.

8:30 Students and parents eat a continental breakfast in the cafeteria.

9:00 Students and parents register for open house.

9:30 The president addresses new students and their parents in the auditorium.

10:00 Morning activities start.

11:30 Students give tours of the campus.

12:00 Professors meet with parents and students at lunch to talk about their classes.

1:00 Dr. Linda Hale lectures about the importance of college today.

2:00 Dr. Ed Mesler leads a discussion about choosing a major.

3:00 Kathleen Henry talks about financial aid.

1. when / students and parents / arrive at the college

   Question: _When will students and parents be arriving at the college?_

   Answer: _They will be arriving at the college by 8:00._

2. when / students and parents / eat breakfast

   Question: _____

   Answer: _____

3. when / students and parents / register for the open house

Question: _____

Answer: _____

4. where / the president / address new students

Question: _____

Answer: _____

5. at what time / morning activities / start

Question: _____

Answer: _____

6. who / give tours / of the campus

Question: _____

Answer: _____

7. what / happen / at lunch

Question: _____

Answer: _____

8. what / Dr. Hale / lecture about

Question: _____

Answer: _____

9. what / Dr. Mesler / lead a discussion about

Question: _____

Answer: _____

10. who / talk about / financial aid

Question: _____

Answer: _____

Practice

Shiva and his mother are at the Woodland College Open House. Complete their conversation with *will* + base verb or the future progressive of the verbs in parentheses.

Shiva: The campus tour (start)

will be starting in a few minutes.
1

Mother: Oh, good. I think I (go) _____
2

on the tour with you.

Shiva: Actually, the schedule says there (be)

_____ two tours at the
3

same time: one for parents and one for

students.

Mother: Oh, ok. Then I guess I (take) _____ the tour for parents.
4

Shiva: (you, go) _____ back to work after that? Or
5

(you, stay) _____ for lunch?
6

Mother: I thought I would go back to work. But now I think I (stay) _____.
7

If I miss lunch, I (not, get) _____ a chance to meet your
8

professors. I'd like to see what professors you (have) _____
9

in the fall.

Shiva: You don't have to stay. I (tell) _____ you about them when
10

I come home.

Mother: I'd really like to stay. In just a few weeks you (go) _____
11

to classes, and I (not, see) _____ you as often.
12

11 Practice

Imagine that you are planning a vacation for the people in the photograph. Tell them where they will be going and what they will be doing at the following dates and times. Use the future progressive. You may use ideas from the list or your own.

check in to hotel   hike in the Grand Pitons

dine by candlelight   lie on a beach

fly to St. Lucia   miss the snow and cold

1. On Saturday, January 15, you

   _____

   at 8:00 A.M.

2. At 11:30 A.M., _____

   _____.

3. _____ by this time tomorrow.

4. _____ in the afternoon.

5. In the evening, _____.

6. _____ at the end of the day.

3e Other Expressions of the Future; The Future in the Past

Student Book p. 74

12 Practice

Complete the sentences using *be to* or *be about to* + the verbs in parentheses.

1. Gabriel Torres (finish)

   is about to finish his latest

   painting.

2. He (paint) _____ the last detail.

3. The painting (be) _____ displayed in a famous art gallery.

4. It (sell) _____ for nearly $50,000.

5. When the painting is sold, the money (help) _____ start an art program for children in New York City.

6. Gabriel (call) _____ his agent and tell him the good news.

7. His agent thinks Gabriel's art career (become) _____ very successful.

13 Practice

Gabriel had just finished his painting when something happened to change his plans. Complete the sentences using *was/were about to* + the verbs in parentheses.

1. Gabriel (paint) _____ the last part when he heard a noise outside.

2. His five-year-old daughter (knock) _____ on the door, but instead, she ran into the room.

3. Gabriel (move) _____ away from the painting. However, surprised by his daughter, he moved toward it. Red paint sprayed on the canvas.

4. His daughter (laugh) _____, but when she saw Gabriel's face, she started to cry.

5. Gabriel's wife came in. She and Gabriel (yell) _____ at their daughter, but they hugged her instead.

6. They (tell) _____ her that she had done something wrong, but they realized she was too young to understand.

7. Gabriel (call) _____ the agent and tell him the painting would not be done, but then he changed his mind.

8. He (start) _____ a new painting, but then he decided that the red paint made the painting more interesting.

14 Practice

For each photo, write three sentences using the prompts and a verb of your choice.

A.

1. (*be to* or *be about to*)

_____

_____

_____ .

2. (*was/were going to* + verb)

_____ .

3. (*plan, intend, decide,* or *mean* + infinitive)

_____ .

B.

1. (*be to* or *be about to*)

_____

_____

_____

_____ .

2. (*was/were going to* + verb)

_____

_____ .

_____ .

3. (*plan, intend, decide,* or *mean* + infinitive)

_____ .

3f The Future Perfect Tense and The Future Perfect Progressive Tense

Student Book p. 77

15 Practice

Melissa is about to graduate. Complete the sentences using the simple present, the future perfect, or the future perfect progressive and the verbs in parentheses.

1. By the end of the day, Melissa (graduate)
   <u>will have graduated</u> .

2. By the end of the ceremony, her parents
   (see) _____
   her receive her diploma.

3. Before she (graduate)

   _____, she

   (practice) _____ the ceremony with her classmates twice.

4. By the end of the ceremony, she (wear) _____

   her cap and gown for two hours.

5. By Sunday, Melissa (attend) _____

   three graduation parties.

6. Also by then, she (receive) _____

   many cards and gifts.

7. Who (her, send) _____ cards

   and gifts?

8. She has many relatives from far away. They (not, come) _____

   _____ by then.

9. By the time she (start) _____ the fall semester at college,

   she (be) _____ away from high school for four months.

10. She (work) _____ for four months before she

    (go) _____ to college.

11. Before she (quit) _____ her summer job, she (save)

_____ her money for college for four months.

12. Hopefully, she (save) _____ at least $1,000 by the end of August.

13. Meanwhile, by this time next year, what (her parents, do) _____ ?

14. They (prepare) _____ for another graduation.

15. Her younger sister (finish) _____ high school by May of next year!

16 Practice

Imagine that you will live to be 100. What do you think you will have done (or not done) by your 100th birthday? Write three sentences using the future perfect and three sentences using the future perfect progressive.

_____

_____

_____

_____

_____

_____

17 Practice

Read these sentences about the future. Write _C_ next to the sentence if the tense is used correctly. Write _I_ if it is used incorrectly.

_____ **1.** How long they will have been traveling in Asia?

_____ **2.** By the end of the summer, my little brother will have been reading 25 books.

_____ **3.** Where will everyone be working after the company closes?

_____ **4.** The mayor is give a speech at 3:00 today.

_____ **5.** Jacob will be attending law school next year.

_____ **6.** Will you be being at home tonight, or are you going out?

_____ **7.** If the painters will have finished by 4:00, they will earn more money.

_____ **8.** The boss won't call you unless there is a problem.

_____ **9.** I am about to call her, but I couldn't find the phone number.

_____ **10.** Elise will have practicing the piano for three hours by the time her parents come home.

SELF-TEST

A Choose the best answer, A, B, C, or D, to complete the sentence. Mark your answer by darkening the oval with the same letter.

1. I will read the book when I
_____ the time.

   A. am going to have Ⓐ Ⓑ Ⓒ Ⓓ
   B. will have
   C. have
   D. am having

2. Hurry up! The class _____ in five minutes!

   A. starts Ⓐ Ⓑ Ⓒ Ⓓ
   B. will have started
   C. starting
   D. will starting

3. Miguel _____ by the time his brother starts high school.

   A. graduated Ⓐ Ⓑ Ⓒ Ⓓ
   B. will graduating
   C. will has graduated
   D. will have graduated

4. They _____ that car, but they decided not to.

   A. are going to buy Ⓐ Ⓑ Ⓒ Ⓓ
   B. are about to buy
   C. will be buying
   D. were about to buy

5. Tom: Oh, no! I left my books in the restaurant.
Lisa: Wait here. _____ them for you.
   A. I get Ⓐ Ⓑ Ⓒ Ⓓ
   B. I'll get
   C. I'm going to get
   D. I'm getting

6. Chris has been driving without a break. He _____ in Ohio by 6:00.

   A. is going to arrive Ⓐ Ⓑ Ⓒ Ⓓ
   B. will arrived
   C. arrives
   D. will arriving

7. Who _____ if you need money?

   A. will you have called Ⓐ Ⓑ Ⓒ Ⓓ
   B. you will call
   C. will you call
   D. are you calling

8. The neighbors _____ back from vacation until Sunday.

   A. aren't coming Ⓐ Ⓑ Ⓒ Ⓓ
   B. are not come
   C. not be coming
   D. aren't going to come

9. By the time Sara _____ the gym, she will have been exercising for two hours.

   A. is leaving Ⓐ Ⓑ Ⓒ Ⓓ
   B. has left
   C. will have left
   D. leaves

10. I can't meet you at 1:00. _____ lunch with my boss at that time.

   A. I'm eat Ⓐ Ⓑ Ⓒ Ⓓ
   B. I'll be eating
   C. I will have eaten
   D. I will have been eating

B Find the underlined word or phrase, A, B, C, or D, that is incorrect. Mark your answer by darkening the oval with the same letter.

1. Jessica <u>is saving</u> all her money <u>because</u>
   <u>A</u>   <u>B</u>

   she <u>will plan</u> <u>to travel</u> in Europe.
   <u>C</u>   <u>D</u>

   Ⓐ Ⓑ Ⓒ Ⓓ

2. <u>Will</u> she <u>has</u> <u>finished</u> the test <u>by the end</u>
   <u>A</u>   <u>B</u>   <u>C</u>   <u>D</u>

   of the class?

   Ⓐ Ⓑ Ⓒ Ⓓ

3. Emily <u>was about to</u> <u>buying</u> the shoes, but
          <u>A</u>   <u>B</u>

   she <u>decided</u> they <u>were</u> too expensive.
       <u>C</u>   <u>D</u>

   Ⓐ Ⓑ Ⓒ Ⓓ

4. The invitation <u>says</u> that the wedding
                   <u>A</u>

   <u>will to</u> <u>begin</u> at <u>exactly</u> 6:00.
   <u>B</u>   <u>C</u>   <u>D</u>

   Ⓐ Ⓑ Ⓒ Ⓓ

5. <u>By the time</u> the baseball game <u>ends</u>, we
   <u>A</u>   <u>B</u>

   <u>will</u> have <u>been spending</u> all our money.
   <u>C</u>   <u>D</u>

   Ⓐ Ⓑ Ⓒ Ⓓ

6. They <u>start</u> the meeting <u>as soon as</u>
         <u>A</u>   <u>B</u>

   everyone <u>has</u> <u>arrived</u>.
            <u>C</u>   <u>D</u>

   Ⓐ Ⓑ Ⓒ Ⓓ

7. <u>What</u> does Ken <u>want</u> to do <u>if</u> he
   <u>A</u>   <u>B</u>   <u>C</u>

   <u>will become</u> president of the club?
   <u>D</u>

   Ⓐ Ⓑ Ⓒ Ⓓ

8. The bus <u>is departing</u> at 9:00 <u>every</u>
            <u>A</u>   <u>B</u>

   morning, and <u>it</u> <u>returns</u> at 3:00 each
                <u>C</u>   <u>D</u>

   afternoon.

   Ⓐ Ⓑ Ⓒ Ⓓ

9. <u>How long</u> <u>they will</u> have <u>been talking</u> by
   <u>A</u>   <u>B</u>   <u>C</u>

   the time they <u>hang up</u> the phone?
                 <u>D</u>

   Ⓐ Ⓑ Ⓒ Ⓓ

10. I <u>predict</u> they <u>are canceling</u> the game <u>if</u>
       <u>A</u>   <u>B</u>   <u>C</u>

    the rain <u>continues</u> all afternoon.
             <u>D</u>

    Ⓐ Ⓑ Ⓒ Ⓓ

UNIT 4 NOUNS AND EXPRESSIONS OF QUANTITY

4a Regular and Irregular Plural Nouns
Student Book p. 90

1 Practice
Complete the sentences with the correct form of the nouns in parentheses.

Yesterday, Daryl took his family to the beach, and they had a great time. There were

(person) _____ playing Frisbee, some (man) _____ were fishing, and
_____1_____   _____2_____

lots of (child) _____ were playing in the sand. The (wave) _____
_____3_____   _____4_____

weren't very big, so there were no (surfer) _____ in the water. Daryl's family sat
_____5_____

in their beach (chair) _____ and laid on their (towel) _____. After a
_____6_____   _____7_____

while, Daryl and his wife walked in the water and got their (foot) _____ wet.
_____8_____

Near the water, some (dog) _____ were chasing some snowy plovers, which are
_____9_____

a kind of bird. They are an endangered (species) _____.
_____10_____

2 Practice
Read the newscast. Circle the correct form of the verbs in parentheses.

In the news today, five people (was / were)
_____1_____
caught trying to break in to a department store

downtown. One woman (was / were) later released,
_____2_____
but the four men (was / were) held at the police
_____3_____
station. The men (is / are) accused of trying to steal
_____4_____
radios, CD players, and laptops. The laptops

(was / were) found in the back of the men's van.
_____5_____
The thieves (hasn't / haven't) spoken to lawyers yet.
_____6_____

Practice

Read these sentences. Write *C* next to the sentence if the noun forms are correct.
Write *I* if the noun forms are incorrect.

———— **1.** Doug is studying physics at school.

———— **2.** When he gets his master's degree, he'll have to write a theses.

———— **3.** He chose that school because it has the best curriculum.

———— **4.** The person in his department are brilliant.

———— **5.** Doug received a memoranda yesterday about his final project.

———— **6.** He's writing a series of articles for a national magazine.

———— **7.** His wife is also a scientist. She studies bacteria in cacti and fungus.

———— **8.** They have a young children.

———— **9.** Their son just got his first tooth.

———— **10.** Doug and his wife hope to get good paying job when they finish their degrees.

4 **Practice**

Complete the sentences with your own words. Use *is* or *are* in your answers.

1. My teeth _____ .

2. The media in my country _____ ,

   so the news _____ .

3. _____ an endangered species in my country.

4. Blue jeans _____ .

5. Businesspeople _____ .

6. A 60-year-old man _____ .

7. Five-year-old children _____ .

4b Possessive Nouns; Possessive Phrases with *Of*

Student Book p. 93

5 Practice

Read the sentences. Answer the questions with
one or *more than one.*

1. **a.** The men's hobbies are expensive.
   How many men have hobbies?
   <u>*more than one*</u>

   b. The man's hobbies are expensive.
   How many men have hobbies?
   _____

2. **a.** The room's furniture needs replacing.
   How many rooms should get new furniture?
   _____

   b. The rooms' furniture needs replacing.
   How many rooms should get new furniture?
   _____

3. **a.** I can't find the child's toys.
   How many children are missing toys?
   _____

   b. I can't find the children's toys.
   How many children are missing toys?
   _____

4. **a.** The boys' projects are almost finished.
   How many boys are almost finished?
   _____

   b. The boy's projects are almost finished.
   How many boys are almost finished?
   _____

5. **a.** The baby's blankets are dirty.
   How many babies have dirty blankets?
   _____

   b. The babies' blankets are dirty.
   How many babies have dirty blankets?
   _____

6. **a.** The students' homework is too difficult.
   How many students have difficult homework? _____

   b. The student's homework is too difficult.
   How many students have difficult homework? _____

6 | Practice

Read the conversations. Rewrite sentence B, adding the possessive noun that is missing.

1. **A:** Whose CD is that?

   B. It's Scott's. _It's Scott's CD_____.

2. **A:** Whose car is that?

   B: It's Leslie's. _____.

3. **A:** Whose responsibility will it be?

   B: It'll be the city's. _____.

4. **A:** Whose turn is it to pay for lunch?

   B: It's Cheryl's. _____.

5. **A:** Whose idea was it to put salt in the sugar bowl?

   B: It was Alex's. _____.

6. **A:** Whose locker was broken into?

   B: Patricia's. _____.

7. **A:** Whose material are you using?

   B: The department's. _____.

8. **A:** Whose database will we be accessing?

   B: Accounting's. _____.

7 | Practice

Use apostrophes or *of* and the words in parentheses to complete the sentences.

My (neighbor, house) _____ caught on fire last night.
                              1

The fire started (in the front, house) _____. The
                                              2

(electrical system, house) _____ was faulty. My neighbor
                                   3

lost (her mother, jewelry) _____ and (her children,
                                   4

photos) _____, but thankfully no one was hurt.
               5

8 Practice

Read these sentences. Write *C* next to the sentence if the apostrophe or *of* is correct. Write *I* if it is incorrect.

_____ 1. Tomorrow homework is to read chapter two.

_____ 2. We will hear Maria presentation.

_____ 3. Let's look at today assignment.

_____ 4. The date of the exam will be announced next week.

_____ 5. The name the next unit is Ancient Greek History.

_____ 6. IT installed the laser jet printer in the corner of the room.

_____ 7. Has Mr. Monroe turned in his letter resignation?

_____ 8. The erosion hillside is now threatening the subdivisions below it.

9 Practice

Write sentences using apostrophes or *of*, the words in parentheses, and your ideas.

1. The (name, this book) is _____.

   The name of this book is Grammar Form and Function .

2. My (best friend, name) is _____.

   _____.

3. My (parent, taste) in clothes is _____.

   _____.

4. My (instructor, name) is _____.

   _____.

5. My (family, last vacation) was _____.

   _____.

6. The (streets, my city) are _____.

   _____.

7. _____ is my favorite (time, the year).

   _____.

8. _____ is the (name, my favorite book).

   _____.

4c Compound Nouns

Student Book p. 97

10 Practice

Match each group of words on the left with the word on the right that fits to make compound nouns.

1. _____ : hat, cut, doll   **a.** water
2. _____ : spray, brush, cut   **b.** car
3. _____ : bulb, switch, pole   **c.** music
4. _____ : graphics, programmer, science   **d.** coffee
5. _____ : mechanic, door, seat   **e.** light
6. _____ : fall, glass, bottle   **f.** paper
7. _____ : lesson, teacher, video   **g.** hair
8. _____ : table, pot, machine   **h.** computer

11 Practice

Complete the sentences with compound nouns using the information.

1. The tour was three hours long. It was a *three-hour tour* _____ .

2. The girl is seven years old. She's a _____ .

3. The semester is 15 weeks long. It's a _____ .

4. Her latest book is 600 pages long. It is a _____ .

5. The flight was 16 hours long. It was a _____ .

6. The meal was three courses. It was a _____ .

7. The bottle of wine cost six dollars. It was a _____ .

8. Our final paper is going to be ten pages long. It's going to be a _____ .

9. We don't have school on Monday. Our weekend will be three days long. It's going to

   be a _____ .

10. That restaurant has four stars. It must be good. It's a _____ .

12 Practice

Underline the compound nouns in the following reading.

Nick had wanted to be a race-car driver ever since he was a seven-year-old boy. In high school, he worked part time as an auto mechanic while he took driving lessons. The day he got his driver's license was the happiest one of his life!

Nick bought an old car and worked on it in his spare time. He started racing other boys on country roads outside town. As he won more and more of these races, he became more and more confident. Pretty soon, Nick applied to drive on a professional racetrack.

The day of the race, there was a rainstorm. Huge thunderclouds made the sky black, and the race was cancelled. Nick was disappointed, but he now had a chance to double-check his car. It was a good thing. During his inspection, he noticed his seatbelt wasn't connected well to the base! If he had raced, it could have been very dangerous.

4d Count Nouns and Noncount Nouns

Student Book p. 100

13 Practice

Read these phrases. Write *C* next to the phrase if the article is used correctly. Write *I* if it is used incorrectly.

_____ **1.** a happiness

_____ **2.** an air

_____ **3.** an experience

_____ **4.** a weather

_____ **5.** an iron

_____ **6.** a glass

_____ **7.** a sunshine

_____ **8.** two sodas

_____ **9.** a hair

_____ **10.** a rice

14 Practice

Read the recipe for brownies. Circle the count nouns. Underline the noncount nouns.

from the kitchen of _____

Brownies

1 teaspoon vanilla

½ cup butter

2 squares of chocolate

¾ cup flour

1 cup of sugar

½ cup nuts

2 eggs

Melt the butter and chocolate together. Remove from heat. Stir in sugar. Add eggs and vanilla. Mix gently until combined. Add flour and nuts. Put mixture in a square cake pan and bake for 30 minutes at 350°.

15 Practice

Circle the correct verbs in parentheses.

1. Geography (isn't / aren't) very interesting to me.

2. Medicine (is / are) a popular major at my university.

3. My new glasses (is / are) already broken!

4. Bad experiences (is / are) a part of life.

5. Chocolate (is / are) good for you.

6. Education (is / are) very important.

7. The good times I had in college (was / were) some of my happiest moments.

8. Time (goes / go) quickly.

9. Gasoline (has been / have been) very expensive lately.

10. The two cups of coffee I had this morning (is / are) making me nervous.

16 Practice

Add two more items to each of the noncount noun lists.

Languages	Natural Forces	Recreation
Portuguese	*wind*	*soccer*
_____	_____	_____
_____	_____	_____

Abstract Nouns	Liquid	Particles
love	*milk*	*sand*
_____	_____	_____
_____	_____	_____

17 Practice

Complete the sentences with *much, many, little,* or *few*.

A. Art Director: You don't have _____ ideas.
1

Artist: I didn't have _____ time to do this. _____
2   3

artists could meet this deadline. I had _____ warning.
4

Art Director: This is an important client. _____ other companies want
5

its business.

B. Mia: My parrot isn't doing _____ talking today.
1

Tawni: Do you think he's depressed? He has very _____ room to walk
2

around in that cage.

Mia: No, this is just his traveling cage. His cage at home is huge.

_____ birds have such luxury!
3

Tawni: Oh, so where's he going?

Mia: To my best friend's apartment. He's gone there _____ times
4

before. He loves to go visit, so he'll probably start talking again once we

get there.

18 Practice

Complete the sentences with your own ideas.

1. Students have too much _____ and too little _____.

2. They have too many _____ and too few _____.

3. Parents have too many _____ and too few _____.

4. In the winter, there is too much _____ and too little _____.

4e *Some* and *Any*

Student Book p. 103

19 Practice

Circle the correct words in parentheses.

Leonard: Come on over. We can get (some / any) Chinese food.
                                              1

Ziggy: There's never (some / any) parking in your neighborhood.
                               2

Leonard: Take the bus. There isn't (some / any) traffic this time of day.
                                       3

Ziggy: Okay. Should I bring (some / any) drinks?
                                 4

Leonard: Well, I have (some / any) bananas and yogurt and was thinking of making
                          5
          (some / any) smoothies.
           6

Ziggy: Okay. How about if I bring (some / any) strawberries? Oh, and I've also got
                                       7
          (some / any) new CDs to show you.
           8

Leonard: Great.

20 Practice

Read these sentences. Write *C* next to the sentence if *some* or *any* is used correctly. Write *I* if it is used incorrectly.

_____ **1.** The team finished the project without some problems.

_____ **2.** The kids still have some homework to do.

_____ **3.** Dr. Walker seldom has any time for hobbies.

_____ **4.** Darlene's lost weight. She hardly has some clothes to wear.

_____ **5.** She needs to buy some new shoes, too.

_____ **6.** We have to water the garden because we haven't had some rain.

_____ **7.** If you have your own business, you rarely take some vacations.

_____ **8.** You can wear my sunglasses. I have any extra ones in the car.

21 Practice

Complete the sentences with *some* if the speaker expects a "yes" answer. Complete the sentences with *any* if the speaker has no expectation.

1. (I need tape, but I don't know if you have tape.)

Do you have __*any*__ tape?

2. (I think you'll let me borrow money.)

Could I borrow _____ money?

3. (Your friend is having a party. You think she needs help.)

Do you need _____ help?

4. (You don't know if your friend has enough food for the party.)

Should I bring _____ snacks?

5. (You don't know if other people from work are going to be at the party.)

Will _____ people from work be there?

6. (Your friend doesn't have enough CDs. You think she would like music at the party.)

Do you want me to bring _____ music?

Practice

Write *a, b,* or *c* beside each sentence to identify which meaning of *any* is being used.

————— **1.** I can meet you any time you like.

————— **2.** There's hardly any tea left!

————— **3.** Our math teacher doesn't have any patience.

————— **4.** Any kind of cake is fine with me.

————— **5.** Are there any more dishes in the sink?

————— **6.** She never has any money.

————— **7.** Did you have any pets growing up?

————— **8.** Jake will take any job he's offered.

a. Negative meaning

b. No expectation

c. It doesn't matter which one

◆ **4f** *Much, Many, A Lot Of, A Few, Few, A Little,* and *Little*

Student Book p. 106

23 **Practice**

Complete the sentences with *a little, a few,* or *a lot of.* More than one answer may be correct.

Anne: My wallet was stolen!

Mike: Did you have ————————————
       1

      money in it?

Anne: No, only ————————————, but I had
       2

      ———————————— pictures and credit
       3

      cards.

Mike: When did this happen?

Anne: Only ———————————— hours ago.
       4

Mike: Have you called the police?

Anne: Yes, I talked to them ———————————— while ago.
       5

Mike: Do you need ———————————— money right now? I can lend you some.
       6

Anne: No, thanks, Mike. I have ———————————— dollars at home.
       7

24 Practice

Complete the sentences with *much, many, a few, few, a little, little,* or *a lot of.*

My nephew is staying with me for the summer, and he's driving me crazy. We're having

_____ problems, not many. He tried doing his laundry and put too
        1

_____ soap in the washing machine. There were bubbles and water everywhere!
        2

He gets too _____ phone calls late at night, and he makes too
                    3

_____ noise. I'm getting very _____ sleep. I still have
        4   5

_____ patience, but I'm left with _____ options. _____
        6   7   8

things are going to have to change.

25 Practice

What does each sentence mean? Answer the questions.

1. I have a few friends.

   Do I have friends? <u>Yes, you have some friends, but not a lot of friends</u>.

2. My brother has few friends.

   Does he have friends? _____.

3. The students have very little time to finish the project.

   How much time do the students have? _____.

4. Very few people are still in the office at this hour.

   How many people are still working? _____.

5. There's a little soap left.

   Can I do laundry? _____.

6. We found a little money in the sofa!

   How much money did they find? _____.

7. The director has made few changes to the proposal.

   Has the proposal been changed a lot? _____.

8. We're having a few friends over for dinner.

   How many people will be at dinner? _____.

Nouns and Expressions of Quantity

4g *Each, Each (One) Of, Every, Every One Of, Both, Both Of, All, and All Of*

Student Book p. 110

26 Practice

Katie bought a new PDA two months ago. Read the paragraph and circle the correct expressions in parentheses.

I have trouble with this thing (each / every)
1
day. (Each / Every) time I use it, I have to restart
2
it. I have spoken to two customer service

representatives, and (each / every) one has told me
3
something different! My husband has the same

machine, and (all of / both of) us are frustrated.
4
(All / Every) my friends love their PDAs and never
5
have any problems with them. Today mine crashed,

and I can't access the information. (Every one of / Each) my addresses is in it. I think I'm
6
going to return (all of / both of) ours to the store.
7

27 Practice

Complete the sentences with *both, every,* or *all*.

1. Sharon's been to that doctor twice. _____ times, he's kept her waiting
   for an hour.

2. _____ time she tries to talk to him, he's busy.

3. He laughed at _____ my jokes, and I told him a lot of them.

4. _____ meal on the menu was too expensive.

5. Our daughter's pet hamster kept us awake _____ night.

6. Luanne can write with _____ hands.

7. When Juan won the lottery, _____ of his money problems disappeared.

8. _____ Alan and Jan have agreed to sign the petition.

9. _____ one of the people in that room was angry.

10. _____ the exercises in the book are easy.

28 Practice

Complete the sentences with your own ideas.

1. Both of my eyes _____ .

2. Both of my parents _____ .

3. All of my friends _____ .

4. Each one of my teachers _____ .

5. Every one of my classmates _____ .

6. Both of my shoes _____ .

7. All children _____ .

8. Every newspaper in my country _____ .

9. Every person needs _____ .

10. All of the people in the world _____ .

SELF-TEST

A **Choose the best answer, A, B, C, or D, to complete the sentence. Mark your answer by darkening the oval with the same letter.**

1. My aunt never had any _____.

   A. childs   (A) (B) (C) (D)
   B. child's
   C. children's
   D. children

2. When Matthew was in high school, mathematics _____ his favorite subject.

   A. was   (A) (B) (C) (D)
   B. were
   C. are
   D. is

3. Last ____ fashions were influenced by hip-hop.

   A. year   (A) (B) (C) (D)
   B. year's
   C. years
   D. of year

4. The neighbors bought a _____ house.

   A. 100-year-old   (A) (B) (C) (D)
   B. 100-years-old
   C. 100-year's-old
   D. 100-year

5. Pollution in the city _____ in recent years.

   A. are decreased   (A) (B) (C) (D)
   B. have decreased
   C. has decreased
   D. were decreased

6. There weren't _____ people injured at the concert.

   A. much   (A) (B) (C) (D)
   B. any
   C. some
   D. few

7. My country has very ____ iron, so we import it.

   A. much   (A) (B) (C) (D)
   B. many
   C. little
   D. few

8. We rarely get ____ rain in the summer here.

   A. much   (A) (B) (C) (D)
   B. many
   C. little
   D. few

9. David works out _____ day.

   A. all of   (A) (B) (C) (D)
   B. every
   C. each
   D. both

10. We can't bake a cake. We have too ____ sugar.

    A. many   (A) (B) (C) (D)
    B. few
    C. a little
    D. little

B   **Find the underlined word or phrase, A, B, C, or D, that is incorrect. Mark your answer by darkening the oval with the same letter.**

1. We can see some <u>sheep</u>, <u>man</u>, <u>women</u>,
                A   **B**   **C**

children, and <u>geese</u> in the painting.
          D

Ⓐ Ⓑ Ⓒ Ⓓ

2. <u>Both of</u> the three plays we saw <u>were</u>
        A   **B**

good. The <u>name of one</u> was *The Time of*
         C

Your Life. It was <u>Ted's</u> favorite.
            D

Ⓐ Ⓑ Ⓒ Ⓓ

3. Mollie took her <u>two-year-old</u> twins on a
                  A

<u>five-hour</u> trip to Boston. <u>Both</u> days that
 B   **C**

weekend, she didn't get <u>some</u> rest.
              D

Ⓐ Ⓑ Ⓒ Ⓓ

4. Al has a <u>driver's license</u>, so he's taking us
               A

to the <u>bookstore</u>. First, I need to get
     B

<u>a little</u> money. We don't have <u>few</u> time.
 C   **D**

Ⓐ Ⓑ Ⓒ Ⓓ

5. They didn't have <u>any</u> oranges at the store,
                  A

so I got <u>some</u> bananas. I also got <u>a few</u>
       B   **C**

cheese and <u>a little</u> juice.
       D

Ⓐ Ⓑ Ⓒ Ⓓ

6. <u>Each people</u> must have a ticket. You
        A

cannot use another <u>person's</u> ticket, but
           B

you can use the same ticket <u>all</u> day. Let's
               C

go over <u>a few</u> rules.
     D

Ⓐ Ⓑ Ⓒ Ⓓ

7. Athletics <u>is</u> an important part of school.
              A

<u>Every</u> <u>student</u> should do <u>few</u> exercise.
 B   **C**   **D**

Ⓐ Ⓑ Ⓒ Ⓓ

8. I'm washing <u>jeans</u>, <u>short</u>, and <u>pajamas</u>.
               A   **B**   **C**

There's <u>a little</u> hot water if you need to
        D

take a shower.

Ⓐ Ⓑ Ⓒ Ⓓ

9. We had a <u>four-hour</u> dinner. <u>Each of us</u> had
               A   **B**

fun, and we told a <u>lot of</u> jokes, but I
            C

don't remember the <u>name's restaurant</u>.
            D

Ⓐ Ⓑ Ⓒ Ⓓ

10. Many <u>exercises</u> in this book <u>is</u> easy, and
            A   **B**

<u>a few</u> exercises <u>are</u> fun.
 C   **D**

Ⓐ Ⓑ Ⓒ Ⓓ

UNIT 5 PRONOUNS AND ARTICLES

5a Subject and Object Pronouns; Possessive Adjectives; and Possessive Pronouns

Student Book p. 120

1 **Practice**

Circle the correct subject, object, possessive pronoun, or possessive adjective.

A. Rich and Sue are discussing their wedding reception.

Sue: Let's put (your / yours) parents next to (my / mine).
                                  1   **2**

Rich: But (my / mine) mother doesn't really know (your / yours).
                          3   **4**

Sue: I know, but I don't know where else to seat (her / hers).
                                                                          5

B. George Washington Carver was the first African American to graduate from what is

now Iowa State University. (He / Him) was responsible for many agricultural
                                          1

innovations and discoveries. One of (them / their) was the invention of peanut butter.
                                                      2

No one (know / knows) exactly when (he / him) was born, but it was around 1865.
                      3   **4**

(He / His) parents were slaves.
        5

C. (She / Her) said that (her / hers) soccer team had just won the championship match.
        1   **2**

The trophy is (their / theirs) for the first time. The team and coaches are already
                          3

planning for next year. (Them / They) want to be sure that the championship trophy
                                      4

stays with (they / them).
                5

D. A wife and husband have just moved into a new house.

Wife: What's (our / ours) new phone number?
                              1

Husband: It's 555-8765.

Wife: No, it's not. That's (our / ours) old one.
                                          2

2 Practice

Complete the sentences with possessive adjectives or pronouns *(my, mine, her, hers, his, our, ours, their, theirs).*

A. Sarah: I don't want any dessert. You can have _____.

                            1

Ryan: Thanks, but I think _____ dessert is going to be enough.

                        2

B. Jenna Lee has just had a job interview. The interviewers are discussing her.

Donna: What did you think of the candidate?

Leroy: _____ ideas are interesting.

             1

Donna: Do you think _____ are better than the other candidates' ideas?

                       2

Leroy: Yes, I do, but I'm not sure we can offer _____ enough money to

                                           3

leave _____ other job.

             4

C. Maureen: When does _____ vacation start?

Jorge: We leave next Saturday.

D. Two children are arguing over a toy.

Pete: Give it back! It's _____.

                     1

Ken: No, it's not! It's _____.

                     2

Mom: Ken! Give it to Pete. It's _____.

                             3

E. Candace and Joyce have _____ own business.

F. Several people are in the reception area of a public relations firm. The new receptionist goes to ask whose clients they are.

Receptionist: Can anyone tell me whose clients are waiting in reception?

Margo and Miriam: The client in the red suit is _____ client. And the client

                                                          1

in the black skirt is Norm and Sara's.

Norm and Sara: Yes, the client wearing red is _____, and the other one

                                                       2

is _____.

          3

G. We have an exchange student from Sweden. I'm learning _____ language,

                                                                     1

and he's learning _____.

                         2

H. Instructor: Please turn off _____ cell phones.
      1

(phone ringing)

Eun Hee: It's not _____ . Marc, I think it's _____ .
                       2   3

Marc: Oops! Sorry. Yes, it's _____ phone.
                                          4

3 Practice

**Read about Komodo dragons.
Complete the sentences with
_it's_ or _its_.**

_____ the largest
          1

lizard in the world. _____
                              2

found on two Indonesian islands.

_____ teeth can tear
          3

easily through flesh.

_____ mouth is filled with bacteria. The infection from a bite can kill
          4

_____ prey. _____ long tongue "tastes" the air. A
          5   6

Komodo dragon starts _____ attack when _____ three
                              7   8

feet away from _____ victim. _____ an interesting,
                       9   10

but ferocious animal.

4 Practice

Answer the questions with _it_.

1. What time is it? _____.

2. What's the weather like? _____.

3. What's the temperature right now? _____.

4. How far is it from your house to your school? _____.

5. How long does it take you to go to school? _____.

6. What's the weather going to be like tomorrow? _____.

5 Practice

Read these sentences. Write *C* next to the sentence if the pronouns and possessive adjectives are used correctly. Write *I* if they are used incorrectly.

_____ 1. It's ours.

_____ 2. The baseball fans forgot his tickets.

_____ 3. Scott critiqued hers project.

_____ 4. Someone took my parking space!

_____ 5. Him's drinking some coffee.

_____ 6. She loves vacations at the beach.

_____ 7. Everyone needs to bring his or her lunch.

_____ 8. Talk to she about the plan.

_____ 9. You can look for apartments online.

_____ 10. Vicky bought the tickets for we.

6 Practice

Read the sentences. Write *a* next to the sentence if the pronoun is formal. Write *b* if the pronoun is informal. Write *c* if the pronoun is inappropriate.

_____ 1. Someone left their lights on.   **a.** formal

_____ 2. Everyone is required to clean out his or her locker.   **b.** informal

_____ 3. Did someone call? Did they leave a message?   **c.** inappropriate

_____ 4. If one has time, one should help others less fortunate.

_____ 5. A good driver has to pay attention to what he's doing.

_____ 6. No one should say things they don't mean.

_____ 7. Everyone should clear his desk now.

_____ 8. A child needs lots of love and support while he or she is growing up.

_____ 9. Anyone can go, but they need to make a reservation.

_____ 10. A good teacher should be sensitive to her students' needs.

5b Reflexive Pronouns

Student Book p. 128

7 Practice

Complete the sentences with the correct reflexive pronouns.

A. If you want something done right, do it _____.

B. Mom: What happened?!

Henry: Freddy and I tried to fix the car by _____. Freddy cut

_____ on a sharp piece of metal, and I burned _____
   2   3

on the exhaust pipe.

Mom: Are you okay?

Henry: Yes, but we can't fix the car _____. We'll take it to a mechanic.
                                        4

C. Carolina: I'm glad you made
it to the party!
Are you enjoying

_____?
      1

Aaron: Of course! I didn't
know anyone here,
so I introduced

_____
      2

to Zoe and Ian.

Carolina: Great. Be sure to help _____ to some cookies. I made
                                        3

them _____.
        4

8 Practice

Replace the underlined words and phrases with *by* and appropriate reflexive pronouns.

1. On the first day of school, the young friends said, "We can walk to school <u>alone</u>."

   On the first day of school, the young friends said, "We can

   walk to school by ourselves."

2. They wanted to walk to school <u>alone</u>.

   _____.

3. Some of the most important lessons we learn in life, we have to learn <u>without others</u>.

   _____.

4. She's doing this exercise <u>alone</u>.

_____.

5. He doesn't want to go to the party <u>alone</u>.

_____.

6. My three-year-old son wants to get dressed <u>without my help</u>.

_____.

7. I don't like living with roommates. I like living <u>alone</u>.

_____.

8. Victor and Carol are nervous about driving to Florida <u>alone</u>.

_____.

9. You are too dependent on your friends. You should do more things <u>on your own</u>.

_____.

10. Father to his two children: Please, go out to the back yard and play <u>with just you two</u>

for a few minutes. _____.

9 Practice

Read the sentences. Circle the correct reflexive pronoun in each. If it is incorrect, rewrite the sentence.

1. I didn't invite him! He invited him! _____ _He invited himself_ _____.

2. Our daughter wrote us from Mexico. She's enjoying herself. _____.

3. Chen cut himself shaving this morning. _____.

4. It's an all-you-can-eat-buffet. Help yourselves. _____.

5. I me will help you. _____.

6. Our dog taught herself how to open the door to the refrigerator. _____.

7. The accident was our fault. We blame us. _____.

8. The children locked themselves in the bedroom. We had to call the fire department.

_____.

9. Anne promised her to quit smoking. _____.

10. Patrick painted the room him. _____.

10 Practice

Complete the sentences with your own ideas and appropriate reflexive pronouns.

1. __I__ don't take care of __myself__ when I __get too busy__ .

2. _____ scared _____ when I _____.

3. _____ surprised _____ when she _____.

4. _____ doesn't look at _____ in the mirror because

   _____.

5. _____ talks to _____ when he _____.

6. _____ drove _____ to the hospital when

   _____.

5c *Another, Other, Others, The Other,* and *The Others*

Student Book p. 130

11 Practice

Read the sentences. Circle the correct words in parentheses.

1. Some students are coming with us, and (other / others) are meeting us there.

2. Sharon: How's your mom?

   Ron: Some days she's okay, but (other / others) days she's very tired.

3. Jasminda: How long does it take you to get to work?

   Miriam: Most days, just 40 minutes on the subway, but (other / others) days it can take an hour.

4. Walter: I'm looking for an apartment. Can you give me some suggestions?

   Brigitte: Some neighborhoods are pretty nice, but (other / others) are not very safe.

5. Stephanie: How's your new boss?

    Paulo: She's okay. Sometimes we work well together, but (other / others) days I don't understand her management style.

6. Flight attendant 1: Your flight was crowded and late arriving to Buenos Aires. How were the passengers?

    Flight attendant 2: Some passengers were calm, (other / others) were angry, and (other / others) were confused.

7. Volunteer 1:   Where have all the donations come from?

    Volunteer 2:   Some have come from religious organizations, (other / others) donations have come from schools, and still (other / others) have come from individual people.

12 | Practice

Complete the sentences with *the other, the others,* or *another*.

1. Mitch is taking five classes. Two are interesting, but _____ aren't.

2. Our team needs _____ week to finish the project.

3. Duane ate one hamburger, then he ate _____, and

_____, and _____!

4. Denise has two neighbors. One is friendly, but _____ isn't.

5. We need _____ $6,000 to finish the house.

6. The company interviewed eight candidates for the positions. Four of them were overqualified, three didn't have the skills we need, but _____ was perfect for the job.

7. Patricia knew some of the students but not _____.

8. The violinist has released a record a year for the last six years. We have two of them but not _____.

13 | Practice

Answer the questions.

1. Underline every other letter.   A B C D E F G H I

2. What's every other day of the week?   Sunday, _____

3. Underline every other year.   1998, 1999, 2000, 2001, 2002, 2003, 2004, 2005, 2006

4. What's every other month in the year?   _____

Practice

Read these sentences. Write *C* next to the sentence if *the other, the others, other, others, every other,* or *another* is used correctly. Write *I* if it is used incorrectly.

———— **1.** We'll be there in the other half an hour.

———— **2.** The players don't get along with each other.

———— **3.** Cost is one reason I can't go to Australia, but there are the others.

———— **4.** Lydia works out every other day.

———— **5.** My mom is one of my heroes, but I have many anothers.

———— **6.** One foot is bigger than the other.

———— **7.** Only 50 guests came to the reception. Some never got their invitations, and others got them late.

———— **8.** Go to bed right now. I don't want to hear another excuse.

5d The Indefinite Articles *A* and *An; One* and *Ones*

Student Book p. 133

15 Practice

Read these sentences. Write *C* next to the sentence if the article is used correctly. Write *I* if it is used incorrectly.

———— **1.** What time is it? I don't have watch.

———— **2.** Did we have an assignment for tomorrow?

———— **3.** Does anyone have a cell phone?

———— **4.** I need to make call.

———— **5.** All living things need an air to breathe.

———— **6.** Grapes cost $0.69 a pound.

———— **7.** Bill works out three days week.

———— **8.** Jessie needs a new wallet.

———— **9.** Before the sales department makes decision, they need more information.

———— **10.** I like to have an apple for breakfast in the morning.

16 Practice

Read the paragraph about Joel. Complete the sentences with _a, an,_ or _one_.

My nephew, Joel, hasn't had _____
1
job in over _____ year. He got
2
_____ call today telling him that he
3
has _____ interview on Thursday.
4
Joel needs _____ haircut,
5
_____ new suit,
6
_____ better résumé, and he only has
7
_____ reference. His interview is at
8
9:00 in the morning, but I'm not sure he has _____ alarm clock. I hope
9
_____ day, he'll be more organized!
10

17 Practice

Rewrite the sentences replacing the repeated nouns with _one_ or _ones_. You may need to make other changes to the articles in the sentences.

1. Sharlene: Don, do you want a soda?

   Don: No, thanks. I already have a soda. _No, thanks. I already have one_.

2. My teacher likes the old designs better than the new designs.

   _____.

3. Vanessa: What's on TV tonight?

   Tom: I don't know. I don't have a TV.

   _____.

4. Sean: Which car did she get?

   Vicky: She got the red car.

   _____.

5. My inbox was filled with messages, so I deleted the old messages.

   _____.

6. Rosa: How was the conference?

Sadiq: It was the worst conference I've ever been to!

_____.

7. Allen: Oh, no! My computer has crashed!

Tyra: Use the computer at the library.

_____.

8. Enrique: How are you doing in your history class?

Tim: Okay. I failed the first test, but passed the other tests.

_____.

9. Salesperson: The earrings on the counter are full price, but the earrings in the basket are on sale. _____

_____.

18 Practice

Think about your future. Start your sentences with "one day."

1. _One day, I'm going to have a house with a pool_ .

2. _____ .

3. _____ .

4. _____ .

5. _____ .

5e The Definite Article *The*
Student Book p. 138

19 Practice

Add *the* to the sentences if necessary. If it's not necessary, don't add anything.

1. Everyone should drink _____ water.

2. _____ water in our city doesn't taste very good.

3. Frank went to _____ store.

4. I got some fruit. Please put _____ bananas on the counter.

5. Ben and his friends are planning a trip to _____ Europe.

6. Look at _____ stars! They're beautiful tonight.

7. Neil Armstrong was _____ first person to walk on _____ moon.

8. My sister's family has a rabbit, a cat, and a dog. _____ rabbit and

_____ dog get along well, but _____ cat doesn't like anyone!

9. Manuel loves _____ animals.

10. _____ animals on our rescue farm get good care.

20 Practice

Read the article about surfing. Cross out *the* whenever it's not necessary.

The surfing originated in the Hawaiian Islands. The first European to record a
‾‾‾   1   ‾‾‾   2   ‾‾‾   3
description of it was the Lieutenant James King. The surfing is called "The Sport of
                       ‾‾‾   4   ‾‾‾   5   ‾‾‾   6
Kings." Hawaiian royalty had beaches and surfboards that were different from everyone

else's. Hawaiian culture had strict rules, but as more and more the Westerners came to
                                                                   ‾‾‾   7
Hawaii, the traditions and culture changed. The surfing on the Hawaii fell off, but never
        ‾‾‾   8   ‾‾‾   9   ‾‾‾   10
died out completely. In the 1850s, surfing began to gain in popularity again.
                         ‾‾‾   11

21 Practice

Complete the sentences with your own ideas.

1. **a.** Japanese is <u>*fun to study*</u> .

   b. The Japanese are <u>*very polite*</u> .

2. **a.** People are _____ .

   b. The people in my city are _____ .

3. **a.** Music is _____ .

   b. The music from Jamaica is _____ .

4. **a.** Pollution is _____ .

   b. The pollution in my city is _____ .

5. **a.** Money is _____ .

   b. The money in my wallet is _____ .

22 Practice

Complete the sentences with *a, an,* or *the*.

1. We're having <u>*a*</u> test next week. <u>*The*</u> test will cover chapters 6, 7, and 8.

2. I need to get _____ new printer. _____ one I have now is too old.

3. Do you know _____ good babysitter? _____ guy we usually call is busy on Saturday.

4. _____ sun was really hot today! Vince got _____ bad sunburn.

5. Leon has to write _____ book report. I've never heard of _____ book he's chosen.

6. We took _____ taxi yesterday, and I left my sunglasses in _____ cab.

7. Bring _____ sweater with you this weekend. _____ nights can be really cold at our cabin.

8. Rachel had _____ problem with her car. The mechanic says _____ problem is in _____ fuel line.

9. Host: Do you have _____ reservation?

   Guest: Yes, _____ reservation is for 7:00 for four people.

23 Practice

Read the recipe for Easy Fruit Salad. Complete the sentences with *a, an,* or *the*.

Easy Fruit Salad

_____ apple
1

_____ banana
2

_____ orange
3

a few grapes

_____ melon*
4

(* or any other fruit you like)

_____ lemon
5

2 Tablespoons of honey or any kind of jam

To make the sauce, squeeze _____ lemon into
6

_____ medium-size bowl. Add _____ honey and mix well.
7   8

To make the fruit salad, cut up _____ apple, _____ melon, and
9   10

_____ banana into _____ bowl. Peel _____ orange and
11   12   13

add it and _____ grapes into _____ fruit mixture. Fold
14   15

_____ fruit and sauce gently together and serve!
16

24 Practice

Write a recipe for something you like to make.
Write a list of ingredients and instructions.

_____

_____

_____

_____

_____

SELF-TEST

A **Choose the best answer, A, B, C, or D, to complete the sentence. Mark your answer by darkening the oval with the same letter.**

1. Everyone has to do _____ own work.

   A. they   Ⓐ Ⓑ Ⓒ Ⓓ
   B. their
   C. our
   D. my

2. My family drives me crazy, but I love _____ all.

   A. them   Ⓐ Ⓑ Ⓒ Ⓓ
   B. theirs
   C. it
   D. we

3. In order to win the contest, you must complete the task by _____.

   A. myself   Ⓐ Ⓑ Ⓒ Ⓓ
   B. yourself
   C. himself
   D. itself

4. The children made the dinner by _____.

   A. ourselves   Ⓐ Ⓑ Ⓒ Ⓓ
   B. yourselves
   C. themselves
   D. herself

5. Al and Matt saw a couple of movies this weekend. One was terrible, but _____ was pretty good.

   A. each other   Ⓐ Ⓑ Ⓒ Ⓓ
   B. another
   C. the other
   D. other

6. Lisa needs to get _____ job. The one she has now doesn't pay enough.

   A. each other   Ⓐ Ⓑ Ⓒ Ⓓ
   B. another
   C. the other
   D. other

7. Naoko's family goes to _____ Netherlands every other year.

   A. an   Ⓐ Ⓑ Ⓒ Ⓓ
   B. a
   C. one
   D. the

8. I've got _____ headache.

   A. an   Ⓐ Ⓑ Ⓒ Ⓓ
   B. a
   C. one
   D. the

9. _____ speak Korean.

   A. They Koreans   Ⓐ Ⓑ Ⓒ Ⓓ
   B. The Koreans
   C. The Koreans people
   D. The people

10. The family took a trip around _____ world.

    A. an   Ⓐ Ⓑ Ⓒ Ⓓ
    B. a
    C. one
    D. the

B   **Find the underlined word or phrase, A, B, C, or D, that is incorrect. Mark your answer by darkening the oval with the same letter.**

1. She's <u>a</u> very skilled manager. She worked
     A

   <u>hers</u> way up by <u>herself</u>. I model my career
     B   **C**

   on <u>hers</u> because she's so successful.
        D

   Ⓐ Ⓑ Ⓒ Ⓓ

2. Please, help <u>ourselves</u>. There's plenty of
                      A

   food for <u>everyone</u>. Ursula made <u>her</u>
                B   **C**

   famous cookies. <u>They're</u> delicious.
                         D

   Ⓐ Ⓑ Ⓒ Ⓓ

3. Let's have <u>the other</u> party soon! Everyone
                  A

   had a good time. The guests helped

   <u>themselves</u> to food and introduced
     B

   <u>themselves</u> to <u>each other</u>.
     C   **D**

   Ⓐ Ⓑ Ⓒ Ⓓ

4. This was <u>a</u> great party! The kids behaved
                A

   <u>themselves</u> and we enjoyed <u>yourself</u>. <u>Other</u>
     B   **C**   **D**

   parties I've been to haven't been much fun.

   Ⓐ Ⓑ Ⓒ Ⓓ

5. I gave <u>herself</u> <u>a</u> headache thinking about
              A   **B**

   it. It's too difficult to solve <u>by myself</u>.
                                       C

   I need help from <u>the others</u> on our team.
                         D

   Ⓐ Ⓑ Ⓒ Ⓓ

6. Can you get me <u>another</u> knife? This <u>one</u> is
                       A   **B**

   dirty. Steve will be late for <u>the</u> dinner
                                     C

   party, but <u>each other</u> will be on time.
                  D

   Ⓐ Ⓑ Ⓒ Ⓓ

7. Jack Campbell bought <u>a</u> tent, <u>a</u> sleeping
                            A   **B**

   bag, <u>the</u> ice chest, and <u>a</u> backpack for his
           C   **D**

   camping trip.

   Ⓐ Ⓑ Ⓒ Ⓓ

8. People speak <u>the Portuguese</u> in Brazil,
                     A

   <u>English</u> in Australia, <u>French</u> in France, and
     B   **C**

   <u>Japanese</u> in Japan.
     D

   Ⓐ Ⓑ Ⓒ Ⓓ

9. Linda has to have <u>the</u> best clothes, <u>a</u>
                         A   **B**

   most expensive jewelry, <u>the</u> biggest car,
                               C

   and <u>the</u> nicest house.
          D

   Ⓐ Ⓑ Ⓒ Ⓓ

10. Michael can play <u>the</u> guitar, <u>the</u> piano,
                        A   **B**

   <u>one</u> harmonica, and <u>the flute</u>.
     C   **D**

   Ⓐ Ⓑ Ⓒ Ⓓ

UNIT 6 MODALS I

6b *Can, Could,* and *Be Able To* to Express Ability

Student Book p. 151

1 Practice

Complete the sentences with *can, could,* or *be able to* in the correct tense. More than one answer may be possible.

1. Karen: Why didn't you go?

   Jim: I (not) _____ find anyone to take my class.

2. Police officer: How did you escape from the locked room?

   Vince: I _____ reach the window, open it a little, and yell

   for help.

3. Boss: _____ (you) stay late tomorrow?

   Assistant: No, I'm sorry. I (not) _____ stay late.

4. Mark: Darla _____ always get reservations at the best

   sushi restaurant in town.

   Jeff: She's lucky. Whenever I call, I (not) _____

   get a reservation for the day I want.

5. The director _____ see you tomorrow at 10:30 A.M.

6. Seth: How (you) _____ reach the top shelf?

   Anita: I _____ reach the top shelf by standing on a

   dining room chair.

7. We _____ (not) get cheap tickets, so we're not going to Europe

   this summer.

8. Jay _____ do back flips off the diving board when he was

   12 years old, but he (not) _____ now.

9. Andrea _____ get another ticket for the fashion show next week,

   so we _____ all go together.

10. Last week, I _____ buy a bunch of books on sale!

2 | Practice

Answer the questions with your own ideas. Write complete sentences in the tenses given.

1. Can you write html code?

   _____.

2. Are you able to wiggle your ears?

   _____.

3. Could you whistle using your fingers when you were a child?

   _____.

4. Are you able to touch your nose with your tongue?

   _____.

5. Could you do magic tricks when you were younger?

   _____.

6. Can't you flip your eyelids inside out?

   _____.

7. Weren't you able to curl your tongue?

   _____.

8. Will you be able to walk on your hands if you practice?

   _____.

9. Won't you be able to change a flat tire if I show you how?

   _____.

10. Couldn't you run fast as a child?

   _____.

3 | Practice

Answer the questions using *can* or *be able to* and your own ideas.

1. The cat's up our tree. How can we get him down?

   You can wait for him to get down by himself. You can call the fire department. You can climb up after him.

2. How can you get in your apartment when you lock your keys inside?

_____ .

3. How will you be able to start your car if the battery is dead?

_____ .

4. How can you call someone if you don't have their number?

_____ .

5. How can you travel globally with very little money?

_____ .

6. How can you decorate your apartment without spending a lot of money?

_____ .

* **Bonus:** In one room there are three light switches. In another
room there are three lights. How can you determine which
switch turns on which light by going into each room only
one time?
Note: There are no holes in the walls, special
tools, mirrors, equipment, or other people to help you.

4 Practice

**Read the paragraph on the Mayans and their accomplishments. Write sentences about
them with _could_ or _were able to_. More than one answer may be possible.**

The Mayans, a group of ancient people that lived in modern
day Mexico, Belize, Guatemala, and Honduras, existed from
about 2000 B.C. to A.D. 1500. At the peak of their civilization,
they were builders, artists, astronomers, farmers, and
mathematicians. They predicted eclipses, studied the planets
and constellations, and understood the lunar cycle. They built
cities, observatories, palaces, ball fields, reservoirs for water
storage, and temples, all without metal tools! They cleared the
jungle to make farmland and grew cotton, corn, beans, and
other vegetables. They developed three calendar systems, including one that has a 360-day
year, and used a writing system which combined pictographs and sound characters.

1. _The Mayans could/were able to tell time_ _____ .

2. _____ .

3. _____ .

4. _____ .

5. _____ .

6. _____ .

7. _____ .

6c *Must, Have To,* and *Have Got To* to Express Obligation and Necessity

Student Book p. 154

Student Book p. 154

5 Practice

Read the rules about driving. Match the verbs on the left with the ideas on the right. Then write sentences using *have to* or *must*.

_e_	**1.** stop completely	**a.**	when you back up
_____	**2.** change oil	**b.**	to change gears
_____	**3.** step on clutch	**c.**	at all times
_____	**4.** turn headlights on	**d.**	every 2,500 miles
_____	**5.** get insurance	**e.**	at red lights
_____	**6.** signal	**f.**	when driving at night
_____	**7.** wear seatbelts	**g.**	when you buy a car
_____	**8.** look behind you	**h.**	before you turn

1. _You must stop completely at red lights_ .

2. _____ .

3. _____ .

4. _____ .

5. _____ .

6. _____ .

7. _____ .

8. _____ .

Bonus Answer: Turn on one switch and let it stay on for an hour or so. Turn it off and flip a different switch. Go into the room with the lights. Find the light that's hot—that one is connected to the first switch. The light that's on goes to the second switch, and the cool light that is off goes with the third switch.

6 Practice

Kate and Pedro are talking about rules in the woodworking class. Complete the sentences with *must, have got to,* or the correct tense of *have to.* More than one answer may be possible.

Kate: Last year, we _____ wear our safety glasses all the time.
1

Pedro: That's Mr. Thompson's strictest rule this year, too. We _____
2

wear them all the time.

Kate: What's the rule about equipment? When I took the class, we

_____ return equipment at the end of each week.
3

Pedro: We _____ return equipment after two days, but next year,
4

we _____ return equipment the same day it's checked out.
5

Kate: Yeah, I've heard the accident rule is changing next year, too. Last year, we

_____ report all accidents within a week. Next year, we
6

_____ report them immediately.
7

Pedro: At least some rules are staying the same! This year in class, each person

_____ keep their work area clean, and next year each
8

person _____ keep their work area clean, too.
9

Kate: That makes sense. I _____ keep my area clean when I took the class.
10

Pedro: It's all just common sense. We just _____ follow
11

Mr. Thompson's instructions. He is very clear about that! And students next year

_____ follow even stricter rules—or else!
12

7 Practice

Read the article about guinea pigs. Then write how to take care of them using *have to, have got to,* or *must.*

Guinea Pigs Make Wonderful Pets!

If you love animals, but have a small apartment, why not get a guinea pig (or two)! Guinea pigs can make wonderful pets. Guinea pigs like company, so think about getting a couple (two females or two males, unless you want lots of baby guinea pigs).

> Guinea pigs are affectionate and easy to take care of. They need vitamin C, vegetables, and clean water every day. Guinea pigs like clean cages, so be sure to clean them every three or four days. Newspaper is fine for the bottom of the cage. Guinea pigs are very gentle creatures; so don't make sudden movements or very loud noises near them. They need a safe place to hide and sleep in their cage. Guinea pigs can live ten years, so if you want one, be sure you can make the commitment to take care of him or her for that long.

1. *You have to be ready to take care of one for about ten years before you get one* .

2. _____ .

3. _____ .

4. _____ .

5. _____ .

6. _____ .

8 Practice

Read the rapid-speech sentences. Write the full forms.

1. "Billy's gotta stop missing so many classes."

   Billy has got to stop missing so many classes .

2. "Sorry, I gotta get going."

   _____ .

3. "What did we hafta do?"

   _____ .

4. "We hatta empty the trash."

   _____ .

5. "Deborah hasta get up at 3:00 A.M. every morning."

   _____ .

6. "Yuichiro and Emiko'll hafta study before they'll be able to do anything else!"

   _____ .

9 Practice

Write sentences using the correct tense of *have to* or *have got to*. Use the hints and your own ideas.

1. What did you have to do today to get ready for school?

brush teeth	get up
get dressed	shower

   a. *I had to get up at 6:00* .

   b. _____ .

   c. _____ .

   d. _____ .

2. What will your friends have to do before they will be able to go on vacation?

arrange for a petsitter	make hotel reservations
book their flights	take their exams

   a. _____ .

   b. _____ .

   c. _____ .

   d. _____ .

3. What did people have to do 200 years ago?

   candles   grow food   horses

   a. _____ .

   b. _____ .

   c. _____ .

4. It's the beginning of the school year. What does Lucy have to do to get ready?

buy textbooks	rent an apartment
find a part-time job	set up her computer

   a. _____ .

   b. _____ .

   c. _____ .

   d. _____ .

6d *Not Have To* and *Must Not* to Express Prohibition and Lack of Necessity

Student Book p. 157

☐10 Practice

Mrs. Devine is taking her son to the opera for the first time. Match her instructions on the left with the ideas on the right.

_____ **1.** We don't have to drive.

_____ **2.** You don't have to wear a tuxedo.

_____ **3.** You mustn't lose the tickets.

_____ **4.** We mustn't be late

_____ **5.** You mustn't have your cell phone turned on.

_____ **6.** You don't have to play a musical instrument

a. A suit is fine.

b. to enjoy the performance.

c. It's standard policy.

d. We're taking a limo.

e. because we won't be allowed in.

f. They're irreplaceable.

☐11 Practice

A father is giving his daughters a lecture about life. Complete the sentences with *have to, not have to,* or *mustn't*.

You _____ always try to tell
               1
the truth. You may not be able to do it all the time,

but you _____ try. You
               2

_____ gossip about others because
     3
that hurts them. You _____ try to
               4
control other people either. You _____
               5
take good care of yourself. You _____
               6
treat other people the way you want to be treated.

You _____ take on too many
    7
projects. You _____ do for others what they can do for themselves.
        8
You _____ forgive other people because it only hurts you if you don't.
    9
You _____ try to make the world a better place.
    10

What are some rules that you live by? Use *have to* or *mustn't* in your answers.

1. _____ .

2. _____ .

3. _____ .

12 ## Practice

Read the paragraph on photography. Complete the sentences with *have to* or *not have to* in the correct verb tense.

When photography was invented,

photographers _____
$\quad\quad\quad\quad\quad\quad$1

hold the exposure for several minutes to

get a clear image. Now, of course, people

_____ use film cameras
$\quad\quad\quad$2

because digital cameras are very convenient.

When you used a film camera, you

_____ keep the back of the camera closed until you developed the
$\quad\quad\quad$3

film. When you bought film, you _____ get the right speed and
$\quad\quad\quad\quad\quad\quad$4

exposure for the light and conditions. Now, if you don't have a camera, you

_____ pay hundreds of dollars for one because there are so many
$\quad\quad\quad$5

disposable ones on the market. In the future, people _____ use film
$\quad\quad\quad\quad\quad\quad\quad$6

at all. Photographers _____ carry so much special equipment. In the
$\quad\quad\quad\quad$7

past, they _____ spend a lot of time developing film in the darkroom.
$\quad\quad\quad$8

In the future, photographers _____ do that either.
$\quad\quad\quad\quad$9

13 Practice

Complete the sentences with your own ideas.

1. Customer service representatives have to <u>*try and help you*</u>, but they don't have to <u>*fix the computer*</u>.

2. Hairstylists have to _____,

   but they don't have to _____.

3. A musician has to _____,

   but he or she doesn't have to _____.

4. Housekeepers have to _____,

   but they don't have to _____.

5. Good friends have to _____,

   but they don't have to _____.

6. A gardener has to _____,

   but she or he doesn't have to _____.

7. Children have to _____,

   but they don't have to _____.

8. A couple has to _____,

   but they don't have to _____.

14 Practice

Read the statements. Circle *Agree* or *Disagree* and explain your answer.

1. You don't have to have a college degree to get a good job.

   (Agree)　　Disagree　　<u>*If you are passionate about something,*</u>
   <u>*you can get a good job without a degree.*</u>

2. Teachers mustn't hit students.

   Agree　　　　Disagree　　_____

3. Students mustn't sleep in class.

   Agree　　　　Disagree　　_____

4. You don't have to have a lot of money to be happy.

   Agree　　　　Disagree　　_____

5. Children mustn't talk to strangers.

   Agree   Disagree   _____

6. You mustn't make sudden moves around wild animals.

   Agree   Disagree   _____

7. People mustn't eat meat.

   Agree   Disagree   _____

8. People don't have to get married to have children.

   Agree   Disagree   _____

9. You don't have to wrap gifts before you give them.

   Agree   Disagree   _____

10. A society doesn't have to have rules.

   Agree   Disagree   _____

6e *Should, Ought To,* and *Had Better* to Give Advice
Student Book p. 159

15 Practice

Read the sentences with *had better* and write the possible consequences. Use *or* in your answers.

1. The class had better leave now, _or they'll miss the bus_ .

2. The children had better not eat so much ice cream, _____ .

3. You'd better be careful working so close to the grill, _____ .

4. My wife and I'd better stop spending so much money, _____ .

5. Jin had better start paying more attention in class, _____ .

6. I think we'd better call a technician, _____ .

7. The gardener had better water the yard today, _____ .

8. I'd better get a job soon, _____ .

9. I'd better work out more, _____ .

10. I had better _____ .

16 Practice

Read the following problems. Write suggestions using *should, shouldn't,* **or** *ought to.*

1. stolen laptop <u>You should call the police and file a report.</u> (OR)
   <u>You should ask if anyone saw anything.</u>

2. depression

   _____ .

   _____ .

3. marital problems

   _____ .

   _____ .

4. a bad haircut

   _____ .

   _____ .

5. forgetfulness

   _____ .

   _____ .

6. high gasoline prices

   _____ .

   _____ .

7. insomnia

   _____ .

   _____ .

8. dyslexia

   _____ .

   _____ .

9. anorexia

   _____ .

   _____ .

10. a haunted house

   _____ .

   _____ .

17 Practice

Read the dialogues. Think of an appropriate situation for the responses.

1. Ryan: *Ellen just yelled at me in front of everyone at my desk.*

   Hideki: That's terrible!

   Rob: You should talk to her supervisor.

2. Jerome: _____.

   Chandra: That's great!

   Peggy: We should celebrate! Let's call everyone.

3. David: _____.

   Elsie: Well, I understand, but I think you should apologize to her.

4. Beth: _____.

   Ed: Really? You should call the police.

5. Michael: _____.

   Deborah: That's too bad.

   Kevin: You should come to the study sessions. They really help me.

6. Marissa: _____.

   Kyle: That looks terrible! You should put a bandage on that.

7. Gerald: _____.

   Krystal: You did? You should ask for a raise.

18 Practice

Read the questions and give advice using *should (not), ought to,* or *had better*.

1. What should someone do to learn another language?

   _____.

2. What should someone do if he or she is in a car accident?

   _____.

3. What should someone do if their computer crashes?

   _____.

4. What should people do if they have a lot of work to do, but they're too tired to do it?

_____ .

5. What should someone do to live a better, healthier life?

_____ .

6f *Should Have* and *Ought To Have* to Express Regret or a Mistake

Student Book p. 161

19 **Practice**

Read the statements with *should have* and *shouldn't have*. Then write the reality or mistake of each situation.

1. They should have told you when they were going to come back.

   They didn't tell you when they were coming back, and now

   you feel it was a mistake .

2. I shouldn't have eaten so many cherries. I don't feel very good right now.

   _____ .

3. We should have spent more time on our presentation.

   _____ .

4. My brother should have returned the library book two days ago.

   _____ .

5. You should have introduced yourself to our new neighbors.

   _____ .

6. Ugh. I just got off the phone with Angie. I should have let the machine pick it up.

   _____ .

7. The homeowners said they shouldn't have left the paint cans so close to the furnace.

   _____ .

8. You argue so much that you should have been a lawyer!

   _____ .

20

Practice

Kija Lee is a reporter. She's asking people on the street about regrets they have. Read their statements and write their regrets.

A. Kija: Excuse me, sir. Could I ask you a question?

   Andy: Sure.

   Kija: Do you have any regrets?

   Andy: Well, I should have gone to college when I had the chance. But I think it's too late now.

   Regret: _Andy didn't go to college_   .

   And last year I gave my wife a vacuum cleaner for her birthday. I shouldn't have done that!

   Regret: _____ .

B. Kija: Ma'am. How about you? Do you have any regrets?

   Ms. Kim: Well, I should have accepted that job in Vietnam. It was a great opportunity.

   Regret: _____ .

   And I shouldn't have started smoking again. It's so hard to quit!

   Regret: _____ .

C. Kija: Excuse me, sir. I'm talking with people about regrets. Do you have any that you'd like to share with our readers?

   Pierre: I should have checked my parking meter earlier. Look! I got a ticket.

   Regret: _____ .

No, but seriously. I should have taken my family to the beach for our last vacation. We rented a cabin in the mountains, and it rained every day, and we were without power for most of the time. It was not fun.

Regret: _____.

D. Kija: Excuse me. Do you have any regrets?

You: I should have _____.

Regret: _____.

And I shouldn't have _____.

Regret: _____.

---

21 Practice

Read the rapid-speech sentences. Write the full forms.

1. "You shoulda been there. It was a riot!"

You should have been there. _____

2. "We better get going."

_____.

3. "Tommy oughta've moved to France."

_____.

4. "We coulda lent you the money."

_____.

5. "Kirk musta gotten lost. Otherwise, he woulda been here by now."

_____.

6. "Do we hafta do this right now?"

_____.

7. "Who shoulda done this?"

_____.

8. "Spock always hasta solve the problems on the ship."

_____.

Read the situations and complete the sentences. Use the words in parentheses and your own ideas. Be sure to use *not* if you write a negative sentence.

1. Yesterday the electric company was working on the utility pole outside my house. This morning when I looked outside, the pole was on fire! Luckily, the fire department came quickly and put out the fire.

    a. The crew (must) <u>*must have done something wrong yesterday*</u>.

    (OR) <u>*They must not have fixed it*</u>.

    b. The fire (could) <u>*could have spread to other houses*</u>.

    c. The crew (should) <u>*should have made sure their work was*</u>

    <u>*finished yesterday*</u>.

2. A young couple moved into the apartment next to me last month. Today I saw the woman packing boxes and carrying suitcases to her car. I haven't seen the man in a while.

    a. They (may) _____.

    b. She (must) _____.

    c. They (should) _____.

3. At Maureen's favorite seafood restaurant yesterday, she tried crab for the first time. She usually has shrimp, but she wanted to try something different. An hour after lunch, Maureen got sick.

    a. She (must) _____.

    b. She (could) _____.

    c. She (should) _____.

4. Zoe is a software consultant. She bills her customers every month. Last month she changed her accounting software, and she hasn't received any checks yet this month.

    a. She (must) _____.

    b. She (should) _____.

    c. She (could) _____.

23 Practice

Answer the questions. Write sentences with *should have* or *shouldn't have*.

1. In your opinion, what is a mistake or decision that your government has made that you disagree with. What should (not) they have done?

   _____

   _____.

2. What is a mistake or decision that your best friend has made that you disagree with? What should (not) he or she have done?

   _____

   _____.

3. What is a mistake or decision that your parents have made that you disagree with? What should (not) they have done?

   _____

   _____.

6g *Be Supposed To* to Express Expectation
Student Book p. 164

24 Practice

Rachel and Yuri are teaching their children table manners. Write sentences with *be supposed to* or *not be supposed to* and the following ideas.

1. put elbows on the table

   You're not supposed to put your elbows on the table .

2. wait until everyone is seated before starting to eat

   _____.

3. chew with your mouth open

   _____.

4. say you don't like something

   _____.

   leave it on your plate

   _____.

5. put your napkin in your lap

_____.

6. cover your mouth and say "excuse me" if you burp

_____.

7. reach across the table to get something you want

_____.

ask someone politely to pass it to you

_____.

What are some other manners that children are taught?

1. _____.

2. _____.

3. _____.

---

25 ## Practice

Read the sentences about Holly and Steve meeting friends at a concert. Write possible ideas for why their plans went wrong. Answer the questions.

1. We were supposed to meet Betty and Mike at 7:00, _but we never met them_.

2. We were supposed to leave our house at 6:00, but _____

_____.

3. They were supposed to call one of us on our cell phones if we missed each other,

but _____.

4. We were supposed to have dinner with them, but _____.

5. There were supposed to be fireworks after the concert, but _____

_____.

6. It wasn't supposed to rain, but _____.

Read the statements. Fill in _T_ if the statement is true and _F_ if the statement is false.

1. Holly and Steve met Betty and Mike at the concert.   Ⓣ   Ⓕ

2. Holly and Steve didn't leave their house at 6:00.   Ⓣ   Ⓕ

3. They all ate dinner together.   Ⓣ   Ⓕ

4. There were fireworks.   Ⓣ   Ⓕ

5. It didn't rain.   Ⓣ   Ⓕ

SELF-TEST

A **Choose the best answer, A, B, C, or D, to complete the sentence. Mark your answer by darkening the oval with the same letter.**

1. The Browns _____ go camping with us.

   A. might could   Ⓐ Ⓑ Ⓒ Ⓓ
   B. may be able to
   C. can to
   D. didn't could

2. Jake _____ move the sofa. He found his keys on the bed.

   A. didn't must to   Ⓐ Ⓑ Ⓒ Ⓓ
   B. must to
   C. have to
   D. didn't have to

3. The firm _____ better sign the contract tomorrow, or they'll miss the opportunity.

   A. had   Ⓐ Ⓑ Ⓒ Ⓓ
   B. have
   C. ought to
   D. should

4. The new law says that drivers _____ block the sidewalk.

   A. must not   Ⓐ Ⓑ Ⓒ Ⓓ
   B. don't must
   C. should to
   D. ought to

5. Theresa _____ returned the phone call, but she didn't get the message until this morning.

   A. had to   Ⓐ Ⓑ Ⓒ Ⓓ
   B. should
   C. should have
   D. was able to

6. The women _____ to meet their trainer at 6:30 A.M.

   A. must   Ⓐ Ⓑ Ⓒ Ⓓ
   B. are supposed
   C. should
   D. had better

7. You _____ told her your opinion. She didn't ask you for it.

   A. didn't have to   Ⓐ Ⓑ Ⓒ Ⓓ
   B. should
   C. could
   D. shouldn't have

8. I think we _____ better compare prices before we decide which DVD player to get.

   A. should   Ⓐ Ⓑ Ⓒ Ⓓ
   B. could
   C. had
   D. must

9. Miriam _____ turn down the oven, but she turned it up instead. Now the pie is burned.

   A. is supposed to   Ⓐ Ⓑ Ⓒ Ⓓ
   B. was able to
   C. was supposed to
   D. had better to

10. Helen _____ email me back, but she did.

    A. mustn't   Ⓐ Ⓑ Ⓒ Ⓓ
    B. didn't have to
    C. had to
    D. supposed to

B **Find the underlined word or phrase, A, B, C, or D, that is incorrect. Mark your answer by darkening the oval with the same letter.**

1. Frankie <u>has</u> finish the paper tonight
   <u>   </u>
      A

   because he <u>won't be</u> <u>able</u> <u>to</u> tomorrow.
          B   **C** **D**

   Ⓐ Ⓑ Ⓒ Ⓓ

2. Karl <u>should</u> <u>have</u> <u>read</u> the directions
       A   **B**   **C**

   before he started playing the game. He

   <u>better</u> take a look at them now.
   D

   Ⓐ Ⓑ Ⓒ Ⓓ

3. Jay <u>shouldn't have</u> accepted the position.
         A

   He <u>can't</u> the job. He'<u>s</u> <u>supposed</u> to tell
      B   **C** **D**

   them tomorrow that he quits.

   Ⓐ Ⓑ Ⓒ Ⓓ

4. I'll <u>have to</u> <u>check</u> my calendar, but we
       A   **B**

   <u>may</u> able <u>to go</u> with you.
   C   **D**

   Ⓐ Ⓑ Ⓒ Ⓓ

5. Someone <u>is</u> supposed <u>come</u> tomorrow to
         A   **B**

   look for the leak. I <u>couldn't</u> climb up
             C

   there, so I <u>can't</u> fix it.
         D

   Ⓐ Ⓑ Ⓒ Ⓓ

6. You <u>should</u> called the architect before we
       A

   left. She <u>was</u> <u>supposed to</u> have the plans
        B   **C**

   ready but she doesn't. Now what are we

   <u>supposed to</u> do?
   D

   Ⓐ Ⓑ Ⓒ Ⓓ

7. Sue and I <u>ought to</u> <u>have</u> <u>went</u> to the gym,
          A   **B**   **C**

   but we <u>couldn't</u> wake up this morning.
         D

   Ⓐ Ⓑ Ⓒ Ⓓ

8. High school students <u>must</u> wear uniforms.
             A

   Girls <u>mustn't</u> <u>wear</u> short skirts, and boys
       B   **C**

   <u>don't must</u> wear jeans.
   D

   Ⓐ Ⓑ Ⓒ Ⓓ

9. You're <u>supposed</u> to offer your seat to the
         A

   elderly. You <u>don't had to</u>, but <u>you</u> <u>should</u>.
           B   **C** **D**

   Ⓐ Ⓑ Ⓒ Ⓓ

10. I <u>can drive</u> here because I have a driver's
      A

    license. Yesterday, I <u>could</u> rent a car. I
              B

    <u>was</u> <u>able to</u> get a good price on it, too.
    C   **D**

    Ⓐ Ⓑ Ⓒ Ⓓ

UNIT 7 MODALS II

7a *Shall, Let's, How About, What About, Why Don't, Could, and Can* to Make Suggestions

Student Book p. 174

1 **Practice**

Edna and Lucy are looking for somewhere to have lunch. Complete the sentences with *how about, what about, shall, could,* or *can*. More than one answer may be possible.

Edna: This place looks interesting.

_____ we have lunch here?
1

Lucy: Okay. _____ just
2

having a light lunch? Then we

_____ go for a run later.
3

Edna: All right. That's a good idea.

They go into the restaurant.

Edna: _____ we sit by the window?
4

Lucy: Definitely. That's a nice view of the bay.

Edna (*to server*):   Hello. _____ sitting near the window? Is that possible?
5

Server: Yes, of course.

Edna: Hmm. I don't know what to order.

Server: Well, _____ trying the special? It's chicken salad, and it has
6

chicken, raisins, and walnuts in it.

Edna: I'm allergic to walnuts. Maybe the chef _____ leave them out.
7

Server: I'm sorry. It's already made. _____ the penne with spring
8

vegetables? It comes with salad and garlic bread.

Edna: That sounds perfect.

Lucy: I'd like the same thing, but I don't really like garlic bread.

Server: I _____ ask the chef to give you plain bread instead.
9

Lucy: Thanks. I'd appreciate that.

Server: _____ something to drink?
                            10

Edna: I'll have iced tea, please.

Lucy: Just water for me, thanks.

2 | Practice

**Read the dialogue between two college roommates. Complete the sentences with *let's,
how about, what about, could,* or *can*. More than one answer may be possible.**

Michele: We have two hours before class. What do you want to do?

Natalie: _How about/What about_ going home and taking a nap?
                            1

Michele: I don't want to do that. _____ do some shopping. We
                                                2

            _____ check out that new shoe store on Pine.
                        3

Natalie: Or, we _____ go to the library and take a nap.
                                4

Michele: Natalie! I don't want to take a nap!

Natalie: Okay, okay. _____ getting some coffee then? I'm really sleepy.
                                5

Michele: Okay. There's a coffee shop next to the shoe store. _____ go
                                                                        6

            there first.

3 | Practice

**The phrases of suggestion in the following sentences are incorrect. Rewrite the
sentences correctly three different ways using *how about, let's,* and *why don't*.
Add question marks if necessary.**

1. _How about turn on_ some music.

    How about turning on some music?   **(OR)**

    Let's turn on some music.   **(OR)**

    Why don't we/you turn on some music?

2. _Why don't order_ a pizza.

    _____

    _____

    _____

3. <u>Let's us meet</u> at my house.

_____

_____

_____

4. <u>Let's not taking</u> the highway.

_____

_____

_____

5. <u>Why don't taking</u> my car.

_____

_____

_____

6. <u>How about we going</u> now.

_____

_____

_____

7. <u>Why we don't take</u> some more time before we decide.

_____

_____

_____

8. <u>Let's we go</u> to the lake this weekend. It's going to be beautiful.

_____

_____

_____

9. <u>How about not play</u> card games for a change.

_____

_____

_____

10. <u>Let's going</u> out for dinner.

_____

_____

_____

4 Practice

A friend doesn't know what to do with his/her future. Write suggestions using *how about, what about, could,* and *why don't.*

You could take classes to find out what you're interested in.

Why don't you make an appointment with a career counselor?

_____

_____

7b *Prefer, Would Prefer,* and *Would Rather* to Express Preference
Student Book p. 176

5 Practice

Complete the sentences with *prefer* or *would rather* and *to* or *than* if necessary.

Laura: I'm thinking about planting vegetables in our garden. What do you think?

Kevin: Really? I _____ have a flower garden.
    ₁

Laura: But we live so far away from the grocery store, I _____ grow my own
    ₂

tomatoes _____ go eight miles. I also _____ the
    ₃   ₄

flavor of fresh vegetables _____ store bought ones.
    ₅

Kevin: Yes, but a vegetable garden takes more time than a flower garden. When I get

home from work, I _____ relaxing _____
    ₆   ₇

watering and weeding the garden.

Laura: You won't have to do anything. I _____ take care of it myself anyway.
    ₈

6 Practice

Complete the sentences on the left with the endings on the right.

_____ **1.** The children prefer water

_____ **2.** Jessica would rather stay home

_____ **3.** The royal family would prefer

_____ **4.** Josh prefers cooking at home

_____ **5.** Samantha would

a. than go to the movies.

b. to eating out.

c. rather eat tofu than seafood.

d. to juice.

e. not to comment on the situation.

7 Practice

Answer the questions with your own ideas. Explain your preferences.

1. Do you prefer to drive or take taxis?

_I prefer to take taxis. I don't like driving_____.

2. Would you rather spend money flying in first class or have the extra money to spend on your vacation?

_____.

3. Would you rather work for someone else or be your own boss?

_____.

4. Do you prefer spicy food to mild food?

_____.

5. When you go out, would you rather listen to a DJ or listen to a live band?

_____.

6. When you eat dinner, would you rather sit at a table or eat in front of the TV?

_____.

7. Do you prefer to work out at the gym or to go for a run outside?

_____.

8. Do you prefer eating at fast-food restaurants to eating at home?

_____.

8 Practice

Write as many questions and answers as you can using *would rather* and *prefer* and the following ideas.

1. history / physics

   - **Q:** _Would you rather study history or physics?_
   - **A:** _I'd rather study physics than (study) history._
   - **Q:** _Do you prefer history to physics?_
   - **A:** _No, I prefer physics (to history)._
   - **Q:** _Do you prefer studying history to studying physics?_
   - **A:** _No, I prefer studying physics (to studying history)._
   - **Q:** _Do you prefer to study history?_
   - **A:** _No, I don't._

2. work with numbers / work with people

3. drive a car / ride a motorcycle

4. gardening / reading

5. talk about your problems with other people / solve them by yourself

_____

_____

_____

_____

7c *May, Could,* and *Can* to Ask Permission

Student Book p. 180

9 Practice

Complete the sentences with *may, could,* or *can.* More than one answer may be possible.

A. James: Excuse me. _____ I take a train schedule?
                                          1

   Clerk: Yes, you _____. Anything else?
                                   2

   James: Yes, _____ I also take the list of fares?
                              3

   Clerk: No, I'm afraid you _____ because there isn't a complete list.
                                                    4

   However, you _____ take anything on the counter.
                                  5

B. Danielle is talking to her best friend.

   Danielle: Claudia? It's me. _____ I talk to you for a minute?
                                                  1

   Claudia: Yes, but I _____ talk for very long. What's up?
                                   2

   Danielle: I need a favor. _____ I use your bike tomorrow?
                                              3

   Claudia: Sure, you _____. Why?
                                   4

   Danielle: Mine has a flat tire, and I need to go by the post office.

   Claudia: No problem. You _____ borrow it anytime you need to.
                                         5

C. Sue: Sean, _____ my sister stay at your apartment for a few days
                           1

   while you are out of town next week? She's in town interviewing.

   Sean: That's fine. She _____ stay there the whole week if she needs to.
                                       2

   Sue: _____ she give your number to people while she's there?
              3

   Sean: Yes, she _____, but she _____ give it to just anyone!
                               4   5

D. Helga: _____ I smoke in here?
                       1

   Host: Sorry, you _____. But you _____ smoke out on the patio.
                               2   3

10 Practice

Write *a* or *b* beside each sentence to identify if the modal is used to talk about ability or permission.

_____ **1.** You may be excused.

_____ **2.** Could I look at your notes?

_____ **3.** Beverly could speak Italian fluently when she was in 6th grade.

_____ **4.** May I speak with you for a few minutes?

_____ **5.** You can have my sandwich. I'm not hungry.

_____ **6.** Cats can see in the dark.

_____ **7.** We can see our house from here!

_____ **8.** Could we sit near the front?

_____ **9.** Dad said we could go with you.

_____ **10.** Phil could easily run a 10K when he was younger.

a. ability

b. permission

11 Practice

Use the prompts to write dialogues with *may, could,* or *can*. More than one modal may be correct.

1. You want to miss class. Ask your teacher. He gives you permission.

   You: Mr. Faber, may I be absent tomorrow? My parents are coming for a visit .

   Mr. Faber: Sure. That's no problem. Just ask someone about the homework .

2. You want to study in the United States. Ask your parents. They give you permission.

   _____ ?

   _____ .

3. Your boss wants you to work late. You have a dentist's appointment at 6:00.

   _____ ?

   _____ .

4. Your best friend wants to borrow your digital camera. The camera is broken.

   _____ ?

   _____ .

5. You want to see the dessert menu. Ask the server. He says "yes."

_____ ?

_____ .

6. Your favorite movie star is sitting at a restaurant. Ask her for an autograph. She says "yes."

_____ ?

_____ .

7. You want to try on a different pair of shoes. Ask the shoe salesperson. He says "yes."

_____ ?

_____ .

7d *Will, Can, Could, Would,* and *Would You Mind* to Make Requests

Student Book p. 184

12 Practice

Read some common questions travelers ask in an English-speaking country. Complete the sentences with *could, would,* or *would you mind*.

1. _____ you tell me how to get to Sutter Street, please?

2. _____ you repeat that? I didn't hear what you said.

3. _____ repeating that?

4. _____ you tell me where the hotel is?

5. _____ you tell me if you have a vacancy, please?

6. _____ telling me where the nearest restaurant is?

7. _____ taking our photo, please?

8. _____ you take our photo, please?

9. _____ hailing a cab for me, please?

13 Practice

Jack is asking his friends to help him move. What do their responses mean? Write *accept* or *decline* next to each answer.

Jack: Hey, guys. Would you guys mind helping me move on Saturday?

1. _____*decline*_____ Walter: No way!

2. _____ Bob: Sure.

3. _____ Sanjay: Sorry.

4. _____ Kenneth: Yeah, okay.

5. _____ Sung Hee: I can't.

6. _____ Erik: No, I'd be happy to.

7. _____ Jerry: Yes, I'll be out of town.

How many people are going to help him move? _____

14 Practice

There are mistakes in the following sentences. Cross out incorrect words and add other words as necessary to correct them.

1. Would you mind ~~turn~~ *turning* down the music?

2. Would you going shopping with me?

3. **A:** Could you work late tonight?

   B: Yes, I could.

4. **A:** Would you picking up some butter?

   B: Sure.

5. Would you mind come with me?

6. **A:** Could you lend me your MP3 player?

   B: No, I couldn't. Sorry.

7. **A:** Would you mind not park there?

   B: Oh, sorry!

8. **A:** Would you helping me with this exercise?

   B: No problem.

15 Practice

Write requests based on the following information.

1. A friend of yours plays guitar. You would like to learn. Ask him/her.

    Could you teach me how to play guitar?

2. You need a ride to work because your car isn't working. Ask a coworker.

    _____

3. You still don't understand the unit. Ask your teacher to postpone the test.

    _____

4. The phone's ringing. You have just gotten out of the shower. Ask your roommate to answer it.

    _____

5. You and your roommate share housework, but he/she hasn't washed his/her dishes in a week. Ask them to.

    _____

6. Your girlfriend/boyfriend always talks during movies. Ask him/her to be quiet.

    _____

7. You need a new pair of glasses. The designer frames you really like cost $500. Ask a friend to loan you some money.

    _____

8. You're going to a party and your roommate has a new sweater that would look GREAT on you. Ask him/her to borrow it.

    _____

9. You are at a café and you need to use the restroom. Ask the clerk for the key.

    _____

7e *May, Might,* and *Could* to Express Possibility

Student Book p. 187

16 Practice

Write *a* or *b* beside each sentence to identify if the modal is used to talk about something that is/was possible or something that is/was impossible.

_____ **1.** I couldn't have gone with you. I had to work.	**a.** possible
_____ **2.** You drove? Jin could have gone with you.	**b.** impossible

_____ **3.** We may need to get gas soon.

_____ **4.** He may have called, and we didn't hear the phone.

_____ **5.** Joon Hee might take some online classes this summer.

_____ **6.** The Leiers could have seen Notre Dame but they went to Versailles instead.

_____ **7.** I couldn't have done it without your help.

_____ **8.** Dr. O'Malley couldn't have driven this morning. His car's still in the driveway.

_____ **9.** The sales team may finish their work by midnight if everything goes okay.

_____ **10.** Sarah thinks she might get an "A" on her next test.

17 Practice

Read the conversations. Answer the questions with *may, might,* or *could* to express possibility in the present.

1. Ana: What has happened to your computer?

Luke: I'm not sure. *It might have a virus.* (OR) *The server could be busy.*

Ana: What are you going to do if it doesn't work?

Luke: _____.

Ana: How are you going to finish the report?

Luke: I don't know. _____.

2. A: Wow. This is a really good salad. What's in it? What do you think?

B: I don't know. _____ or

_____.

3: A: How are you going to decorate your new home?

B: I'm not sure, yet. _____ in the living room,

but _____ in the bedrooms.

And _____ in the kitchen.

A: How about the back yard?

B: That's a problem. It's so big. _____.

4. A: How does that magician float in air?!

B: I don't really know, but _____.

5. A: I dreamt I was walking through a green room, and when I looked out the window,

I saw my best friend sitting in a tree waving at me. What do you think it means?

B: I have no idea, but _____ or

_____.

18	Practice

Answer the questions in two ways. Use *may, might,* or *could* + *have* + a past participle to express possibility in the past.

1. A: Why didn't Paige call you back last night?

B: _She might not have had time_ . (OR) _She could have been_

too busy last night .

2. A: Why didn't our English teacher assign any homework yesterday?

B: _____.

_____.

3. A: What has happened to Michael? He looks terrible.

B: I don't know. _____.

_____.

4. A: Do you know why Pedro quit his job last week?

B: _____.

_____.

5. A: Why did Karina start smoking again last summer?

B: _____ .

_____ .

6. A: Why didn't Nikki introduce herself to you at the party?

B: _____ .

_____ .

7. A: Whoa! Did you see that? I wonder why that car ran the red light!

B: _____ .

_____ .

8. A: Have you seen Cheryl? Why has she cut her hair so short?

B: _____ .

_____ .

19 Practice

Read the questions. Answer them with your own ideas. Use *may, might,* or *could +
***have* + a past participle to express possibility in the past.**

1. How was Stonehenge built? Who built it?

It could have been built by druids or ancient priests.

It might have been built by aliens (just kidding!).

2. How did the dinosaurs become extinct?

_____

_____

3. How was the universe created?

_____

_____

Think of some other mysteries. Write possible explanations for them.

4. _____

_____

5. _____

_____

6. _____

_____

7f *Should* and *Ought To* to Express Probability

Student Book p. 192

20 Practice

Complete the sentences with the verbs in parentheses. Use *should/ought to* + base verb for things that are probable in the present or future. Use *should/ought to* + *have* + past participle for things that were probable in the past.

1. They're working hard. They (feel) <u>*ought to feel/should feel*</u> exhausted at the end of their shift.

2. We just ate an hour ago! You (not, be) _____ hungry yet.

3. I gave the baby some medicine. She (stop) _____ coughing by now.

4. Roberto is really tired. He (sleep) _____ well tonight.

5. Lourdes bought the shoes last week. She (try) _____ them on already.

6. There was no traffic this morning. You (not, be) _____ late to the meeting.

7. We're going to a four-star restaurant. The food (taste) _____ superb, and the atmosphere (encourage) _____ diners to relax.

8. Your car used to be in good condition. You (sell) _____ it last year.

9. Mr. Potter (return) _____ soon. He just went to get a cup of coffee.

10. George (not, fail) _____ the exam. He'd studied most of the weekend!

Practice

Complete the sentences about things that have probably happened using the perfect modal form of *should* or *ought to* (*should* or *ought to* + *have*) and the verbs in parentheses.

1. The wedding is in 30 minutes. The flowers (arrive) _should have arrived/_
   ought to have arrived by now.

2. Ann left the job over a month ago. They (post) _____
   the position.

3. Sam: Your cousin's knee was injured the last time I saw her.

   Bob: Yes, she (have) _____ knee surgery, but I haven't
   heard anything.

4. I mailed the package two weeks ago. You (receive) _____
   it by this week.

5. Let's go to the mall. It's late. The crowd (die down) _____.

6. Lucy and Bill are leaving on the 12th. They (get) _____
   their tickets by now.

7. Have you heard anything from the police? They (finish) _____
   the investigation.

8. Barbara is going on a diving trip next week. She (take) _____
   scuba diving lessons by now.

22 Practice

Read the sentences and use your own ideas to tell why the speaker uses *should* or *ought to* + a base verb or *should/ought to* + *have* + a past participle.

1. The opera is in 10 minutes. The audience ought to be seated by now.

   Normally at an opera, the audience arrives and is seated about

   15 minutes before the opera begins. We expect this.

2. The students started the test 90 minutes ago. They should have finished by now.

   _____

   _____.

3. The trip from downtown only takes 40 minutes. They ought to be back any time now.

   _____

   _____.

4. It's 9:30. The mail shouldn't arrive until noon.

   _____

   _____.

5. Let's call Jim. He shouldn't have left yet. It's only 7:30.

   _____

   _____.

6. Today, we should hear if the agent has accepted our offer on the new house.

   _____

   _____.

7. After your massage, you should feel pretty good.

   _____

   _____.

8. We're starting with advanced digital modeling. You should have learned the basics last semester.

   _____

   _____.

7g *Must, Must Not,* and *Can't* to Make Deductions

Student Book p. 194

23 Practice

Write *a* or *b* beside each sentence to identify if *can* or *can't* is used to talk about permission or deduction.

_____ 1. Can I use your computer?

_____ 2. No, you can't.

_____ 3. She left five minutes ago. She can't have gone too far.

_____ 4. My children can only watch five hours of television a week.

_____ 5. This bill can't be right. The waiter forgot to add on our dessert.

_____ 6. Everyone can go to the museum today. It's free on Thursdays.

_____ 7. That clock can't be right. My watch says it's 1:20.

_____ 8. This coat can't be yours. Yours is on the floor over there.

_____ 9. Can I adopt a dog, please?

_____ 10. We can't adopt a dog until we have more time to spend with him or her.

a. permission

b. deduction

24 Practice

Complete the deductions with *must* or *must not* and the ideas in parentheses.

1. That man is calling for help! He (know how to swim) _must not know how to swim_.

2. Everyone in that family has their own car. They (have a lot of money) _____.

3. Cindy has two dogs, three cats, and a canary. She (love animals) _____

_____.

4. I'm waving at Sherry, but she's not waving back. She (see us) _____

_____.

5. Toni screamed when she saw the spider. She (be afraid of them) _____

_____.

6. Jennifer's always upbeat. She (worry too much about small issues) _____

_____.

7. Tom and Danny haven't said two words to each other. They (be angry at each other)

_____.

8. Franklin never suggests we go to science fiction films. He (enjoy science fiction)

_____.

Complete the sentences with your own ideas.

9. This kitchen has everything! The people living here _____

_____.

10. You've finished this exercise already? Modals _____

_____.

25 **Practice**

Match the sentences on the left with the past deductions on the right.

_____ **1.** Carl is dancing. I can't believe it!

_____ **2.** Oh, no. The dog threw up on the living room carpet.

_____ **3.** There's an ambulance across the street at the neighbor's.

_____ **4.** Kevin got directions off the Internet, but he's not here yet.

_____ **5.** My alarm didn't go off, and there are no lights.

a. Something must have happened.

b. The power must have gone off.

c. She must have eaten something that upset her stomach.

d. He must have taken lessons.

e. He must not have followed them correctly.

26 Practice

Read about Armand in high school and now. Write one deduction about the present using *must* and one about the past using *must have* or *must not have*.

In high school

1. Armand weighed 210 pounds.

2. He didn't date anyone in particular.

3. He moved to Seattle after graduation.

4. His twin sister went to the same high school.

5. Armand wore glasses.

6. He was quiet and shy.

Now

1. Armand weighs 190 pounds.

2. He's wearing a wedding ring.

3. He's looking for a house in his hometown.

4. His twin sister is not at the reunion.

5. Armand doesn't wear glasses.

6. He is talking to everyone and smiling a lot.

1. *Armand must work out regularly* .

(OR) *Armand must have started working out* .

2. _____ .

(OR) _____ .

3. _____ .

(OR) _____ .

4. _____ .

(OR) _____ .

5. _____ .

(OR) _____ .

6. _____ .

(OR) _____ .

27 Practice

Read Lucinda's schedule for yesterday. Read the conversation and complete the sentences with *can't have* or *couldn't have* and the verbs in parentheses. More than one answer may be possible.

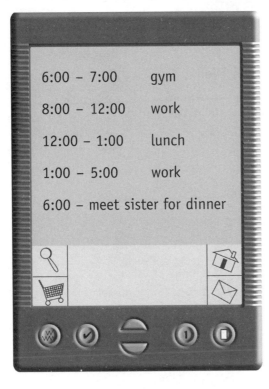

6:00 – 7:00	gym
8:00 – 12:00	work
12:00 – 1:00	lunch
1:00 – 5:00	work
6:00 – meet sister for dinner	

Paulo: Hey, Lucinda! I saw you at the deli yesterday around 11:30.

Lucinda: You (see) _can't have seen_ (OR) _couldn't have seen_ me, Paulo.
1
I was at work.

Paulo: Really? Well, I saw you again outside the bank at 1:30. I waved at you.

Lucinda: That (be) _____ me. I was at work then, too.
2
You (wave) _____ at me.
3

Paulo: I did! And you smiled back.

Lucinda: I (smile) _____ at you. I wasn't there!
4

Paulo: That's strange. You even said "hi."

Lucinda: I (say) _____ anything. Wait a minute.
5
Was 'I' wearing blue jeans?

Paulo: I think so.

Lucinda: Of course! You must have seen my twin sister, Linda.

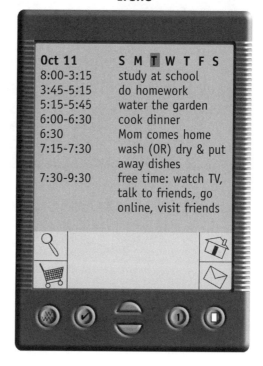

28 Practice

Read about Carole, Irene, and Ellen. Then write sentences about Irene and Ellen's schedule for this Tuesday using *should* or *could* in the progressive form.

Carole has two teenage daughters, Irene and Ellen.
Irene and Ellen help around the house.
These are Irene and Ellen's schedules for this Tuesday.

Ellen

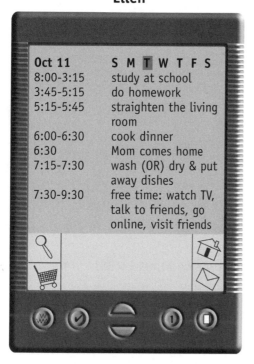

Oct 11	S M **T** W T F S
8:00-3:15	study at school
3:45-5:15	do homework
5:15-5:45	straighten the living room
6:00-6:30	cook dinner
6:30	Mom comes home
7:15-7:30	wash (OR) dry & put away dishes
7:30-9:30	free time: watch TV, talk to friends, go online, visit friends

Irene

Oct 11	S M **T** W T F S
8:00-3:15	study at school
3:45-5:15	do homework
5:15-5:45	water the garden
6:00-6:30	cook dinner
6:30	Mom comes home
7:15-7:30	wash (OR) dry & put away dishes
7:30-9:30	free time: watch TV, talk to friends, go online, visit friends

1. It's 4:00, so Irene and Ellen

  _should be doing their homework_____.

2. It's 5:30, so Irene _____.

3. From 5:15 to 5:45, Ellen _____.

4. At 6:00, Irene _____,

  or Ellen _____.

5. Then, from 7:15 to 7:30, Irene _____.

6. At the same time, Ellen _____.

7. From 7:30 to 9:30, they _____, _____,

_____, or they _____.

29 Practice

It's Saturday. Carole is telling a friend about Irene and Ellen's responsibilities last Tuesday. Write sentences using *should* or *could* in the perfect progressive form.

1. Last Tuesday at 2:45, Irene and Ellen _should have been studying at school_.

2. At 3:45, they _____.

3. At 5:20, Ellen _____.

4. At the same time, Irene _____.

5. At 6:00, Irene _____,

or Ellen _____.

6. At 7:15, Ellen _____.

7. At 8:00, they _____, _____,

_____, or they _____.

30 Practice

You are sitting on a bench on the boardwalk at the beach. Complete the sentences with a modal *could, should, may, might,* or *must* in the progressive or perfect progressive form and the verbs in parentheses. More than one possibility is possible.

1. A woman is carrying a surfboard. She (walk) _could/may/might be walking_

to the beach.

2. Her hair is wet, and she's wearing a wetsuit. She (surf) _____ earlier.

3. She seems tired. She (carry) _____ her surfboard for a while.

4. She stops. She (look) _____ for her jeep.

5. There are also two boys running past you. They (race) _____

to the end of the boardwalk.

6. They are really out of breath! They (run) _____ all the way

from the other end of the boardwalk.

7. The boys are slowing down. They (stop) _____.

8. They are laughing. They (have) _____ a great day at the beach!

31 Practice

Read the sentences about teenagers in a car accident. Write _C_ if the progressive or perfect progressive form is correct. Write _I_ if the progressive or perfect progressive form is incorrect.

_____ **1.** Those kids shouldn't have been standing so close to the highway.

_____ **2.** They could have been waited for a ride.

_____ **3.** Chao and Belinda must not have been hanging out with them.

_____ **4.** We should going to visit them in the hospital.

_____ **5.** They might be waiting for visitors.

_____ **6.** They must not have been paid attention to the cars.

_____ **7.** The police said the traffic light may not have been working correctly.

_____ **8.** They must have been talked loudly. They didn't hear the car coming.

_____ **9.** The doctor said they should be doing well in a couple of days or so.

32 Practice

Complete the sentences with your own ideas.

1. Instead of watching TV, I should be _helping my dad paint the basement_.

2. Instead of doing homework, I could be _____.

3. I should be _____

instead of writing email.

4. Tonight at 6:30, I might be _____.

5. Instead of going to school, I could be _____.

6. One year after I graduate, I might be _____.

7. Instead of spending money, I should be _____.

SELF-TEST

A **Choose the best answer, A, B, C, or D, to complete the sentence. Mark your answer by darkening the oval with the same letter.**

1. _____ we meet at the theater? We can go out to eat after the movie.

   A. Let's   Ⓐ Ⓑ Ⓒ Ⓓ
   B. Why don't
   C. How about it
   D. Let's not

2. We _____ stop by the ATM before we get to the restaurant.

   A. let's   Ⓐ Ⓑ Ⓒ Ⓓ
   B. why don't
   C. how about
   D. could

3. Bill prefers seeing movies on a big screen _____.

   A. than rent them   Ⓐ Ⓑ Ⓒ Ⓓ
   B. to rent them
   C. or rent them
   D. to renting them

4. Our management team _____ keep as many people as possible than let them go.

   A. prefers   Ⓐ Ⓑ Ⓒ Ⓓ
   B. would prefer
   C. would rather
   D. rather

5. A: Could we park here for just a minute?
   B: _____.

   A. Yes, you could   Ⓐ Ⓑ Ⓒ Ⓓ
   B. No, you couldn't
   C. No, you mayn't
   D. Yes, you can

6. _____ not smoking here? I'm allergic to cigarette smoke.

   A. Could you   Ⓐ Ⓑ Ⓒ Ⓓ
   B. Can you
   C. Would you mind
   D. Would you

7. Luckily, no one was home when the tree fell on the house. Someone _____ hurt.

   A. could have been   Ⓐ Ⓑ Ⓒ Ⓓ
   B. should have been
   C. may have been
   D. must have been

8. Toru _____ have paid for dinner. He left his wallet at home!

   A. shouldn't   Ⓐ Ⓑ Ⓒ Ⓓ
   B. can't
   C. may not
   D. could

9. _____ I borrow your car? I'll be very careful, I promise.

   A. Would   Ⓐ Ⓑ Ⓒ Ⓓ
   B. Will
   C. Shall
   D. Could

10. _____ he'll get the computer to work before we leave.

    A. Maybe   Ⓐ Ⓑ Ⓒ Ⓓ
    B. May be
    C. Might be
    D. Would be

B Find the underlined word or phrase, A, B, C, or D, that is incorrect. Mark your answer by darkening the oval with the same letter.

1. Buddy <u>would rather</u> <u>stay</u> inside <u>than</u>
          A   **B**   **C**

   <u>playing</u> outside with other children.
    D

   Ⓐ Ⓑ Ⓒ Ⓓ

2. Suzie <u>would rather</u> <u>having</u> more time off
          A   **B**

   <u>to</u> <u>working</u> a lot.
    C **D**

   Ⓐ Ⓑ Ⓒ Ⓓ

3. My grandson <u>maybe</u> sleeping, or he <u>could</u>
              A   **B**

   be playing music. He <u>should</u> be <u>thinking</u>
                    C   **D**

   about his future!

   Ⓐ Ⓑ Ⓒ Ⓓ

4. We <u>could</u> <u>go</u> to a spa, or <u>what about</u> <u>take</u>
       A **B**   **C**   **D**

   a bike trip through wine country?

   Ⓐ Ⓑ Ⓒ Ⓓ

5. It's five? They <u>should be</u> <u>arrived</u> by now.
                A   **B**

   We <u>could have</u> <u>given</u> them a ride, but they
         C   **D**

   wanted to walk.

   Ⓐ Ⓑ Ⓒ Ⓓ

6. You <u>can</u> <u>have seen</u> me at the carnival
        A   **B**

   yesterday! I was working at home.

   <u>Maybe</u> you <u>saw</u> me the day before.
    C   **D**

   Ⓐ Ⓑ Ⓒ Ⓓ

7. I don't know what's wrong. <u>Maybe</u> he
                          A

   fainted. He <u>could be</u> <u>had</u> a heart attack.
            B   **C**

   The ambulance <u>should be arriving</u> soon.
                D

   Ⓐ Ⓑ Ⓒ Ⓓ

8. She <u>would prefer</u> <u>have</u> the gold one <u>to</u>
         A   **B**   **C**

   the silver one.
    D

   Ⓐ Ⓑ Ⓒ Ⓓ

9. You <u>should</u> <u>of</u> come! Everyone was there.
         A   **B**

   I <u>could have</u> <u>picked</u> you up.
      C   **D**

   Ⓐ Ⓑ Ⓒ Ⓓ

10. Jeanine must have <u>been</u> <u>sleeping</u> when I
                  A   **B**

    called. She <u>prefers</u> <u>sleep</u> late on Saturdays.
            C   **D**

    Ⓐ Ⓑ Ⓒ Ⓓ

UNIT 8 THE PASSIVE VOICE, CAUSATIVES, AND PHRASAL VERBS

8a   The Passive Voice: Overview
Student Book p. 212

1   Practice

Read the sentences. Write *A* next to the sentence if it is in the active voice. Write *P* if it is in the passive voice.

_____ 1. My cousin owns a garage.

_____ 2. Recently, I took my car there for repairs.

_____ 3. In the past, I had been charged too much money by another garage.

_____ 4. In addition, other damages to the car were caused by those mechanics.

_____ 5. My car was fixed by my cousin himself.

_____ 6. However, I was shocked when I saw the bill.

_____ 7. I had been charged even more money by my cousin!

_____ 8. I wasn't given a family discount at all!

2   Practice

Read the sentences. Write *N* next to the sentence if the agent (with a *by* phrase) is needed because it is important to the writer's meaning. Write *U* if the agent is unnecessary or unimportant.

_____ 1. Camera film is made by the Cameramatics Company.

_____ 2. The company was founded in 1961 by a man named Leonard Jameson.

_____ 3. Recently, the company's sales have been hurt by the increase in sales of digital cameras.

_____ 4. Digital cameras are being used more often by people.

_____ 5. Thirty-five millimeter cameras are gradually being replaced by digital cameras.

_____ **6.** In digital cameras, photos are saved on small disks by people.

_____ **7.** At Cameramatics, 200 employees were laid off by Mr. Jameson last month.

_____ **8.** A hundred more employees are going to be dismissed by the new manager next month.

_____ **9.** Many other changes have been made by the company's executives lately.

_____ **10.** A new marketing strategy will be announced by the marketing department at the end of the week.

3 | Practice

Rewrite the following paragraphs in the passive voice where appropriate. State the agent in a _by_ phrase only when necessary. Use the correct verb tense and change object/subject pronouns if necessary.

A.

Welcome to Island Tours! We have a few guidelines to give you. First, we request passengers to carry their identification at all times. We also expect passengers to take their boarding passes with them whenever they leave the boat. If anyone loses their boarding pass, we will charge them a $15.00 replacement fee. Finally, we ask passengers to be very careful on the upper deck. Deck hands have just washed the upper deck. The wood is very slippery right now.

_____

_____

_____

_____

_____

_____

_____

_____

_____

B.

Yesterday, Lars Larsen won the cross-country skiing championship. This is the third year that the champion skier from Norway has won the race. But two days ago, no one believed Lars would win this race. He had injured his left knee six months before the big event. He had surgery on that knee in October. Early in this race, the knee injury troubled Lars. Many people thought he was going to drop out of the race. However, thousands of fans in Norway encouraged Lars. Hundreds of people came all the way to Utah to support him in this race. Lars said that his fans motivated him to win. After a while, he forgot the pain. He passed a rival skier, Italy's Marco Bernini. Once again, the race officials awarded Lars the Golden Ski.

_____

_____

_____

_____

_____

_____

_____

_____

_____

C.

Major floods have destroyed much of Watertown, Ohio. The problems began last week when heavy rains raised the water level in the river. In addition, construction in the area had already damaged the river wall. The town made great efforts to stop the flooding. People built walls out of sandbags all along the river. But the rains continued, and the river water continued to rise and move towards the town. People boarded up windows of homes and businesses. They moved important belongings to the rooftops. Eventually, most residents vacated homes. The National Guard relocated people to shelters in nearby towns. Helicopters took some people from their rooftops and flew them to the shelters. The flood caused nearly $3 million in damage. The town will request emergency aid from federal funds.

_____

_____

_____

_____

_____

_____

_____

_____

_____

The Passive Voice of Modals and Modal Phrases

Student Book p. 219

4 Practice

Read about Mrs. Ellis. Complete the sentences with the words in parentheses and the passive modal or passive perfect modal. Pay attention to time words and phrases. Some sentences refer to the past, some refer to the present, and others refer to the future.

1. In the evenings, our elderly neighbor, Mrs. Ellis, (can, find) _can be found_ watching TV in her living room.

2. She (can, see) _____ eating alone and looking at old photographs.

3. We think her family (should, tell)

   _____ that she needs help in order to live on her own.

4. They (ought to, inform) _____ about this problem a long time ago.

5. The grass outside of Mrs. Ellis's house (has to, cut) _____ soon; it is very tall and full of weeds.

6. The garbage bins by the garage (must, empty) _____.

7. They (must not, empty) _____ for a month or more.

8. The windows and curtains (ought to, wash) _____.

9. In fact, they (ought to, wash) _____ last spring.

10. When we talked to Mrs. Ellis yesterday, she said her carpets (be supposed to, clean) _____ last week, but the cleaning service never arrived.

11. She also said the telephone company (has to, pay) _____ a while ago, but she couldn't find her checkbook.

12. She worried that her phone service (could, disconnect) _____ next month if she doesn't pay her bill.

13. I hope Mrs. Ellis's family (will, inform) _____ about these problems in the near future.

14. Otherwise, I think Mrs. Ellis (had better, move) _____ to a different home where people can help her live independently.

5 Practice

Read the sentences. Write *C* next to the sentence if the passive modal is used correctly. Write *I* if it is used incorrectly.

_____ 1. This mess had better clean by this time tomorrow.

_____ 2. You are going to be charged for the doctor's appointment that you missed.

_____ 3. The rules of the road must obeyed by all drivers.

_____ 4. The homework should had been returned today, but the teacher hadn't finished grading it.

_____ 5. The job might be given to someone with more experience.

_____ 6. Yesterday's soccer game had to cancelled because of the rain.

_____ 7. The order might be shipped as early as Wednesday.

_____ 8. The plane can't been delayed by weather; the weather was perfect in Florida today.

8c The Passive Voice with *Get; Get* + Adjective

Student Book p. 222

6 Practice

Read about Rosa. Use *get* + words from the list to complete the missing information. Use the correct tense. Use "delivered" twice.

bored	involved
delivered	married
depressed	older
divorced	scared
excited	tired
exhibited	worried
hurt	younger at heart

My great-aunt Rosa just turned 80, but she isn't

sad about it. In fact, she never _gets depressed_.
                                          1

She says that while she _____ in
                                          2

actual years, she also _____. She has friends who stopped being
                                    3
interested in new things when they turned 70. They stopped exercising, and as a result,

their energy level went down — they _____ more easily. Rosa
                                                4
says that if people don't try to stay interested and involved in life's activities,

they _____ in their later years. In contrast, Aunt Rosa
                    5
_____ about the next decade of her life. To celebrate her birthday,
            6
she bought a motor scooter. Her children _____ when Rosa first
                                                        7
told them that she wanted to buy a scooter. They _____ that she
                                                                8
would have an accident and that she would _____. Rosa was
                                                        9
never scared. The only time she worried was when the scooter did not

_____ on time.
            10
    What else does Rosa do to stay active? Just recently, she _____
                                                                        11
with a hiking group for seniors. She also works with an organization that helps children

with cancer. She makes teddy bears that _____ to
                                                    12
children in hospitals all over the world. She makes pottery, and some of her work

_____ at an arts and crafts show next month. She enjoys the
            13
company of her new husband. She _____ last year, at age 79!
                                            14
Before that, she had been married for thirty years, but she and her previous husband

_____.
            15

7 | Practice

Look back at the numbered sentences in Practice 6. Write *B* for the sentences in which *get* means *become*. Write *O* for sentences with other meanings of *get*.

1. _B_   6. _____   11. _____

2. _____   7. _____   12. _____

3. _____   8. _____   13. _____

4. _____   9. _____   14. _____

5. _____   10. _____   15. _____

8 Practice

Write at least four sentences about each emotion pictured. Use *get* + an adjective in the present: what do you do when you have this emotion? Then use *get* + an adjective in the past. Write about a time when you had this emotion. What happened?

Example: *I get anxious when I have to speak in public.*
When I get worried about that, I bite my nails.
I got really scared once when I was in a school play.

1.

_____

_____

_____

_____

_____

2.

_____

_____

_____

_____

_____

3.

_____

_____

_____

_____

_____

8d *It* + a Passive Voice Verb + a *That* Clause

Student Book p. 226

9 Practice

Rewrite the sentences in two ways. The first time, use *it* + a passive voice verb + a *that* clause. The second time, use the subject of the active *that* clause as the subject of another passive sentence.

1. People say that my friend Luke is a genius.

   It is said that my friend Luke

   is a genius.

   My friend Luke is said to be

   a genius.

2. The newspaper reported that his software company is the most successful new business of the year.

   _____

   _____

3. Economists estimate that his sales will double next month.

   _____

   _____

4. Consumers believe his products are changing people's lives.

   _____

   _____

5. Everyone knows that starting a new business is difficult in today's economy.

   _____

   _____

6. People think Luke is especially successful because he is only twenty-seven!

   _____

   _____

10 Practice

Write six sentences with *it* + a passive voice verb + a *that* clause. Choose from verbs in the list.

believe	fear	report
confirm	hope	think
consider	know	
estimate	mention	

Example: war

It is feared that this war will not end soon.

1. teenagers today

_____

2. the planet Mars

_____

3. college

_____

4. cigarettes

_____

5. movies

_____

6. yoga

_____

8e Present and Past Participles Used as Adjectives

Student Book p. 228

11 Practice

Read the movie review. Circle the correct adjectives in parentheses.

REVIEW: Danger Zone a Bore ★ ☆ ☆ ☆ ☆

The new movie *Danger Zone* was supposed to be the blockbuster of the summer, but it

was (disappointed / (disappointing)). In fact, I felt so (disappointed / disappointing) by it
      1   2

that I almost walked out before it ended! First of all, the movie — despite its

(exciting / excited) title — is really very (bored / boring). Nothing happens for the first
      3   4

twenty minutes of the movie. Then the story gets (confused / confusing) when we are
                                                           5

suddenly introduced to four new characters. These characters seem (interested / interesting)

                                                                                              6

at first because they are all very different from each other. But I was

(surprising / surprised) when the characters went away, never to be seen again. The

              7

special effects in the movie are (impressive / impressed). Clearly a lot of money was spent

                                              8

on this part of the film. The car chase that went from the streets of New York into outer

space was (amazing / amazed), although it went on a bit too long. By the end of that

                9

scene, I was actually (amusing / amused), but I think the director wanted the audience to

                                  10

feel (frightening / frightened). The worst part of the movie is that it is over two hours

          11

long. It was (exhausted / exhausting) to watch the whole thing from beginning to end. I

                    12

think they could have cut ninety minutes off of this movie, and it might have been more

(interested / interesting) as a result. It certainly wouldn't have been as (tired / tiring)

                13   14

to watch!

12 | Practice

Write about a time in your life when you felt confused, embarrassed, exhausted, or relaxed. Use at least eight present and past participle adjectives. You may tell your story in the past or the present.

Example: *On my first day of classes at my new school, I was very confused. I couldn't understand my schedule, and I was embarrassed when I went to the wrong class. The map of the school was also confusing, and I got lost several times...*

_____

_____

_____

_____

_____

_____

_____

_____

8f Causative Sentences with *Have, Get,* and *Make:* Active Voice

Student Book p. 231

13 | Practice

Gloria and her new roommate, Alison, disagree about what they should have done to the apartment. Read their conversation. Rewrite the causative sentences using *have, make,* or *get* and the words in parentheses. Pay attention to tenses. More than one answer may be possible.

Alison: White walls are depressing. My brother is a painter. I think we should (my

brother, paint) <u>*have my brother paint* (OR) *get my brother to paint*</u>

them purple and blue. I (him, paint) _____ my
2

last apartment, and it looked great. He would be happy to do it for us.

Gloria: The landlord won't let us paint the walls. We'll never (him, agree)

_____ to it. I'm sure he would (us, repaint)
3

_____ the walls white.
4

Alison: Did these curtains come with the apartment? I have a friend who's an

interior designer. I'd like to (her, replace) _____ them
5

with newer ones.

Gloria: My mother made those curtains for me. I like them. I can't (her, take)

_____ them down.
6

Alison: Do you think we can (the neighbors, move) _____
7

those bicycles off of their balcony? They aren't very nice to look at.

Gloria: I don't think so. Their bikes were stolen last year. They (the landlord, give)

_____ them permission to keep their bikes there.
8

Alison: I don't like cleaning. I think we should (a housekeeper, clean)

_____ the apartment once a week.
9

Gloria: I can't afford it. I've never (anyone, clean) _____
10

my apartment for me.

Alison: I'll pay for it. I'll (you, see) _____ how much nicer it
11

is to (someone else, do) _____ the work!
12

8g Causative Sentences with *Have* and *Get:* Passive Voice

Student Book p. 234

14 Practice

Use the prompts to write one causative sentence in the passive voice with *get* or *have*. Then rewrite the sentence in the active voice (See section 8f, Student Book p. 231). Use the tense specified and pay attention to the structure with *get* in the active voice.

1. simple present: I / always / prescriptions / fill / same pharmacy

   a. *I always get/have my prescriptions filled at the*

   same pharmacy.

   b. *I always get the same pharmacy to fill my prescriptions.*

   (OR) *I always have the same pharmacy fill my prescriptions.*

2. present perfect: Linda / her résumé / edit / a career counselor / a few times this year

   a. _____ .

   b. _____ .

3. present progressive: Noel / checks / cash / bank

   a. _____

   _____ .

   b. _____

   _____ .

4. simple present: James / usually / hair / cut / a family friend

   a. _____ .

   b. _____ .

5. simple past: Sandy / nails / paint / her favorite manicurist / last Friday

   a. _____

   _____ .

   b. _____

   _____ .

6. modal: Rachel / should / teeth / look at / the dentist / soon

a. _____ .

b. _____ .

7. present perfect: Midge / her cat / just / check / Dr. Neuman

a. _____

_____ .

b. _____

_____ .

8. simple past: Maryam / laundry / do / the laundromat / last week

a. _____ .

b. _____ .

9. future with *will*: I / will / my apartment / redecorate / an interior designer / next summer

a. _____ .

b. _____ .

10. present progressive: Ellen / film editing program/ explain / Marcus

a. _____

_____ .

b. _____

_____ .

---

15 | Practice

What things would you get someone to do for you, or have done for you, if you were in these situations? What would you NOT have done for you? Write two sentences for each of the following situations, one positive and one negative.

Example: *If I were very wealthy, I would get someone else to do my hair and makeup for me.*
I wouldn't have bodyguards follow me around.

1. if you were very wealthy

_____ .

_____ .

2. if you were 100 years old

_____.

_____.

3. if you were a famous movie star

_____.

_____.

4. if you were a parent of quintuplets (five babies at once)

_____.

_____.

5. if you were the teacher of this class

_____.

_____.

◆ 8h Phrasal Verbs

Student Book p. 236

| 16 | **Practice**

Complete the sentences with particles from the list. You'll use them more than once.

about	on
across	out
down	over
into	up
off	with

Jason and Tina have been dating for almost a year, but last week they nearly broke

_____*up*_____ when they went on a long bike ride together. They had been planning
　　　1

this trip for months, working _____ in the gym to prepare for the 100-mile
　　　　　　　　　　　　　　　　2

ride. But the day of the big ride, Jason showed _____ late to pick
　　　　　　　　　　　　　　　　　　　　　　　3

_____ Tina at her house.
　　　4

On the way to the starting point of the big ride, they ran _____ a friend
5
who said it was supposed to rain. Sure enough, as soon as they showed _____
6
at the starting point of the ride, they learned that the ride might be called

_____ or put _____ because of the weather. Jason and Tina realized
7   8
they had left _____ their rain gear when they packed their bags. At last, it
9
stopped raining, and the riders took _____.
10

About ten miles into the ride, Tina's tire hit a rock, and she fell _____.
11
When Jason helped her get _____, she realized her knee was hurting. She didn't
12
want to give _____ after they had worked so hard to get there, so she put a
13
bandage _____ her knee and went _____. Ten miles later, Jason's
14   15
bike broke _____. He used his cell phone to call _____ a bike
16   17
mechanic for help.

By this time, all the other riders had passed them. They looked _____ the
18
map to make sure they were going the right way. But soon they realized they were lost.

Jason started to complain. Tina told him to get _____ it; that there was
19
nothing they could do. Maybe someone would give them a ride. Maybe they could get

dropped _____ at the starting point. She said she couldn't put up
20
_____ his complaining anymore. Jason told her she should just finish the ride
21
herself. Tina told him to grow _____.
22

Then they agreed to stop arguing and to ride a few miles more. They came

_____ a road with a sign directing the bicyclists. They went _____
23   24
the road and found other bicyclists. When they finally finished the 100-mile ride, they

were so happy that they forgot they had thought _____ quitting!
25

17 Practice

Reread the sentences in Practice 16. Write _S_ if the phrasal verb is separable. Write _I_ if it is inseparable.

1. ___I___   9. _____   17. _____

2. _____   10. _____   18. _____

3. _____   11. _____   19. _____

4. _____   12. _____   20. _____

5. _____   13. _____   21. _____

6. _____   14. _____   22. _____

7. _____   15. _____   23. _____

8. _____   16. _____   24. _____

                                                       25. _____

18 Practice

Rewrite each sentence two ways. Use appropriate pronouns if necessary. If the sentence cannot be rewritten because the phrasal verb is inseparable, write _inseparable verb_.

1. John picked Emily up after work.

   John picked her up after work .

   John picked up Emily after work .

2. They are going to tear down that old building.

   _____ .

   _____ .

3. Everyone stood up while the national anthem was sung.

   _____ .

   _____ .

4. Where should I drop off the books?

   _____ ?

   _____ ?

5. I don't know how to set up my new computer.

_____.

_____.

6. When the war broke out, many families left the country.

_____.

_____.

7. Somebody used up all the sugar.

_____.

_____.

8. Let's get dressed up and go into the city!

_____.

_____.

8i Prepositions Following Verbs, Adjectives, and Nouns; Other Combinations with Prepositions

Student Book p. 244

19 Practice

Complete the sentences with phrases and expressions from the list.

according to	disappointed with	impact on	shouting at
complained about	essential to	need for	solution to
contribute to	fight for	opposed to	tired of
cost of	fond of	responsible for	

Teenagers and their parents in our neighborhood have spoken of a ___*need for*___ a

                                                                            1

community center for young people. Such a center would greatly _____

                                                                       2

the health and growth of our community. Right now, many young people are

_____ the town. They feel that there isn't anywhere for them

              3

to go after school or on weekends. They are _____ going to

                                                          4

the local fast-food place, and the people in the community aren't very

_____ seeing them there all the time either. Local merchants

have _____ the large number of young people that wander up
                    6

and down the street. They are always _____ them to move
                                                7

away from their stores or to go somewhere else.

One _____ this problem would be to build a teen
                    8

center. _____ studies in social psychology, teens that have
                    9

somewhere to go and regularly scheduled activities feel more positive about their lives.

Teens participating in activities at a center also learn positive ways to make an

_____ a community and to create positive change in
                    10

their world.

Of course, the _____ a teen center isn't cheap. And
                                    11

who would be _____ paying those costs? We would. Now, it's
                                12

true that many people may be _____ the idea of using their
                                                13

tax dollars to build this center. But a teen center is _____
                                                                        14

the well-being of our young people, and it is something that we should

_____.
                    15

SELF-TEST

A **Choose the best answer, A, B, C, or D, to complete the sentence. Mark your answer by darkening the oval with the same letter.**

1. He went to the garage to _____.

   A. have his car repaired Ⓐ Ⓑ Ⓒ Ⓓ
   B. have to repair his car
   C. make his car repaired
   D. his car have repaired

2. The family _____ when they heard a noise downstairs.

   A. got scared Ⓐ Ⓑ Ⓒ Ⓓ
   B. getting scared
   C. got scarey
   D. gets scared

3. Which is the passive causative sentence?

   A. Dr. Battaglia has just Ⓐ Ⓑ Ⓒ Ⓓ
   vaccinated Maria's dogs.
   B. Maria has just had Dr. Battaglia vaccinate her dogs.
   C. Maria has just gotten her dogs vaccinated by Dr. Battaglia.
   D. Maria has just gotten Dr. Battaglia to vaccinate her dogs.

4. The taxi _____ by a famous actor.

   A. driven Ⓐ Ⓑ Ⓒ Ⓓ
   B. drove
   C. be driven
   D. was driven

5. The teacher _____ be quiet.

   A. couldn't made the Ⓐ Ⓑ Ⓒ Ⓓ
   students
   B. couldn't make the students
   C. couldn't the students make
   D. couldn't to make the students

6. All customers _____ that the store is closing next month.

   A. will tell Ⓐ Ⓑ Ⓒ Ⓓ
   B. are going to tell
   C. been told
   D. will be told

7. _____ my father, I would like to accept this award in his name.

   A. In behalf of Ⓐ Ⓑ Ⓒ Ⓓ
   B. Of behalf
   C. On behalf of
   D. With behalf of

8. She _____ whenever she reads the newspaper.

   A. gets depressed Ⓐ Ⓑ Ⓒ Ⓓ
   B. depressing
   C. be depressed
   D. depressed

9. Don't _____ any longer; it's due tomorrow morning.

   A. the homework put off Ⓐ Ⓑ Ⓒ Ⓓ
   B. put off the homework
   C. off put the homework
   D. put the homework

10. Katrina _____ her blood pressure tomorrow.

    A. is getting her doctor Ⓐ Ⓑ Ⓒ Ⓓ
    check
    B. is having her doctor to check
    C. is getting her doctor to check
    D. is having checked

B   **Find the underlined word or phrase, A, B, C, or D, that is incorrect. Mark your answer by darkening the oval with the same letter.**

1. <u>It is said</u> that students learn more <u>when</u>
      A   **B**

   they are <u>interesting</u> <u>in</u> the subject.
               C   **D**

   Ⓐ Ⓑ Ⓒ Ⓓ

2. Because <u>so many</u> students <u>failed</u>, the
             A   **B**

   exam <u>given</u> again <u>by the teachers</u>.
        C   **D**

   Ⓐ Ⓑ Ⓒ Ⓓ

3. The plane <u>wasn't arrived</u> <u>on time</u> because
             A   **B**

   <u>there were</u> snowstorms <u>in the Midwest</u>.
     C   **D**

   Ⓐ Ⓑ Ⓒ Ⓓ

4. She <u>couldn't concentrate</u> <u>in</u> her work with
          A   **B**

   all the <u>irritating</u> noise <u>in the room</u>.
        C   **D**

   Ⓐ Ⓑ Ⓒ Ⓓ

5. We tried <u>to get</u> <u>refunded our money</u>, <u>but</u>
         A   **B**   **C**

   we weren't <u>successful at</u> it.
           D

   Ⓐ Ⓑ Ⓒ Ⓓ

6. This piece <u>must</u> <u>had been</u> <u>painted</u> by a
         A   **B**   **C**

   famous and <u>talented</u> artist.
          D

   Ⓐ Ⓑ Ⓒ Ⓓ

7. All employees <u>should</u> <u>informed</u> <u>about</u> the
           A   **B**   **C**

   new rules and <u>go over</u> the handbook.
            D

   Ⓐ Ⓑ Ⓒ Ⓓ

8. <u>It is believed</u> <u>that</u> most car accidents
    A   **B**

   <u>happen</u> when drivers <u>get tire</u>.
    C   **D**

   Ⓐ Ⓑ Ⓒ Ⓓ

9. We were <u>surprised</u> and <u>worried</u> when the
         A   **B**

   police <u>made</u> us <u>to leave</u> the building.
       C   **D**

   Ⓐ Ⓑ Ⓒ Ⓓ

10. The winner <u>will been</u> notified <u>next week</u>
            A   **B**

    and <u>told</u> where to <u>pick up the prize</u>.
       C   **D**

    Ⓐ Ⓑ Ⓒ Ⓓ

UNIT 9 GERUNDS AND INFINITIVES

9a Gerunds as Subjects and Objects; Verbs Followed by Gerunds

Student Book p. 256

1 Practice

Write _G_ next to the sentence if the underlined word is a gerund. Write _V_ if the underlined word is a verb.

_____ **1.** <u>Learning</u> a new language takes a lot of effort and practice.

_____ **2.** I am <u>taking</u> French classes at a language school.

_____ **3.** For me, <u>speaking</u> French is very difficult.

_____ **4.** I really enjoy <u>writing</u> in French.

_____ **5.** <u>Practicing</u> French is difficult because I can't find people to speak it with.

_____ **6.** Recently, however, I have been <u>practicing</u> French with a friend from my class.

_____ **7.** We are <u>trying</u> to talk in French for an hour every week.

_____ **8.** I can't wait to go <u>shopping</u> in France someday and use my French there!

2 Practice

Complete the sentences with the gerund form of verbs from the list.

be	give up	learn	snowboard	swim
exercise	go	ride	stand	take
fall	keep	ski	surf	travel

My friends recently persuaded me to go ___*snowboarding*___ with them up in the
                                            1
mountains. I didn't want to go. I can't stand _____ cold. I like
                                                            2
warm weather and water sports, so I prefer going _____ in a pool
                                                                3
or _____ in the ocean. Also, I had never even gone
            4
_____ before, so I could not imagine _____
            5   6
down a mountain with my feet strapped to a single piece of wood!

Nevertheless, last weekend I found myself _____ up to the
                                                          7

mountains with my friends. They said that _____ a private lesson
                                                          8

was the best way to learn how to snowboard. _____ my balance on the
                                                                     9

board was hard, and _____ down over and over again was painful. I
                                   10

considered _____. However, by the end of the day, I was standing on
                             11

the board and going down small hills by myself. I realized that _____
                                                                                        12

on a snowboard wasn't that different from _____ a surfboard. I enjoyed
                                                          13

_____ how to do a new sport, but I think I still enjoy
            14

_____ in the warm weather more!
            15

3 Practice

Circle the correct form of the words in parentheses.

Sofia enjoys (reads / (reading)) Harry Potter
                            1

novels. She couldn't resist (buying / buy) the latest
                                          2

one as soon as it was (publishing / published). She
                                                3

has almost (finishing / finished) the most recent
                          4

book, but she doesn't (wanting / want) to finish it.
                                    5

She can't imagine (leave / leaving) the characters of
                                6

Harry, Hermione, and Ron and (wait / waiting) until
                                                7

the next book to find out what happens.

(Discuss / Discussing) the Harry Potter novels with
          8

her friends is one of Sofia's favorite things to do.

They are always (argue / arguing) about which book is the best. Tonight they are all
                    9
(go / going) to see the newest Harry Potter movie. People say that this movie (is / being)
       10   11
even better than the last one. Sofia (enjoys / enjoying) the Harry Potter movies, but she
                                              12
prefers (read / reading) the books. She also (hoping / hopes) that the author,
            13   14
J. K. Rowling, will keep on (writing / write) these novels. She can't imagine not
                                 15
(read / reading) about the continuing adventures of Harry and his friends.
     16

4 | Practice

Use each of the following gerunds as the subject of a sentence about yourself or about people you know. Then use each gerund as the object in a sentence.

Example: **a.** (subject) *Dancing is difficult for my boyfriend.*

                b. (object)   *My boyfriend doesn't enjoy dancing very much.*

1. dancing

   a. _____

   b. _____

2. listening (to)

   a. _____

   b. _____

3. studying

   a. _____

   b. _____

4. traveling

   a. _____

   b. _____

5. watching

   a. _____

   b. _____

6. cooking

   a. _____

   b. _____

9b Gerunds as Objects of Prepositions; Gerunds after Certain Expressions

Student Book p. 260

5 Practice

Read the sentences and circle the correct prepositions in parentheses.

1. My friends and I are looking forward (in / at / to) having our spring break.

2. We plan (in / on / to) going to Four Flags Amusement Park.

3. Most of us are interested (on / in / about) going on the new roller coaster there.

4. However, one of our friends, Kim, says that the ride will be a waste (in / at / of) time and money.

5. Kim heard that the lines for the roller coaster are very long, so she says there's no point (in / of / for) standing in a long line to go on a short ride.

6. However, she won't stop us (for / on / from) going on the ride if we want to.

7. She has plans (in / for / on) going shopping while we wait in line for the ride.

8. She says she isn't good (at / in / on) standing in line in the hot sun.

6 Practice

Describe yourself as a student. Answer the questions using gerunds after the prepositions and expressions. Write your answers in complete sentences.

Example: *These days I am busy studying for the TOEFL.*

1. What are you busy doing these days?

   _____

2. What do you have difficulty doing?

   _____

3. What don't you have trouble doing?

   _____

4. What else are you good at doing?

   _____

5. What are you tired of doing?

_____

6. What do you think is a waste of time doing?

_____

7. Has a teacher ever stopped you from doing something? What was it?

_____

8. What is something you look forward to doing soon?

_____

9c Verbs Followed by Infinitives
Student Book p. 263

|7| **Practice**

Mrs. Torres is leaving for work. Her husband and son are saying goodbye. Rewrite the sentences using the verbs in parentheses. Remember that some verbs need objects and some pronouns may need to change. In some cases, more than one answer may be possible.

1. Mr. Torres said, "I'll make breakfast for Alex." (agree)

Mr. Torres agreed to make breakfast for Alex.

2. Mrs. Torres said, "Alex, don't forget to brush your teeth after breakfast." (remind)

_____

3. Alex said, "Please bring me a picture of your office, Mom." (ask)

_____

4. Mrs. Torres said, "Be good and do everything your father asks." (tell)

_____

5. Alex said, "Please come home early." (want)

_____

6. Mrs. Torres said, "I'll call you and Dad at lunch." (promise)

_____

7. Alex said, "Maybe I can watch TV while Mommy is at work!" (hope)

_____

8. Mrs. Torres said to her husband, "Don't let him watch more than one hour of TV." (warn, not)

_____

9. Mr. Torres said to his wife, "You'll be back home by 5:30, right?" (expect)

_____

10. Mrs. Torres said, "Call Kevin next door if you need any help." (encourage)

_____

8 Practice

Read the sentences. Write _C_ next to the sentence if an infinitive is used correctly. Write _I_ if it is used incorrectly.

_____ **1.** The sign warned people to walk not on the grass.

_____ **2.** Her parents didn't permit her to date boys until she was eighteen.

_____ **3.** The neighbors threatened to called the police about the noise.

_____ **4.** Mr. Johnson was asked to move his car, but he refused do it.

_____ **5.** Can you manage to move all those boxes by yourself, or do you want someone to help you?

_____ **6.** We invited him to come on the camping trip, but his parents wouldn't allow him to go.

_____ **7.** Students who can't afford pay the tuition are advised apply for financial aid.

_____ **8.** Some colleges encourage students studying in another country for one semester or longer.

9d Verbs Followed by a Gerund or an Infinitive

Student Book p. 265

9 | Practice

Hannah and Joseph are driving to a national park and have gotten lost. Read their conversation. Circle the correct form of the words in parentheses. Circle both forms if they mean the same thing.

Hannah: I think we should continue

((driving) / (to drive)) until we find a
                1
gas station. When we find one, we

can stop (asking / to ask) for
                2
directions to the national park.

Joseph: We don't need to stop

(driving / to drive). I don't like (asking / to ask) for directions – I'm sure
        3   4
we've just made a simple mistake. We should try (reading / to read) this map
                                                              5
and figure out where we are.

Hannah: I regret (telling / to tell) you that you're looking at the wrong map. I forgot
                        6
(bringing / to bring) the Vermont map with us. This is a map of another state.
        7

Joseph: Then I guess we'll have to remember (planning / to plan) our trip back in April.
                                                          8
Do you recall what road we were supposed to take?

Hannah: No. But now I think I know what happened. We forgot (getting / to get) off the
                                                                      9
highway at Exit 24.

Joseph: I remember (seeing / to see) the sign for Exit 24. But that was about fifteen
                        10
miles back! This is why I hate (traveling / to travel) in such rural areas.
                                              11

10 Practice

Complete the email message with the gerund or infinitive form of the words in parentheses. In some cases, either a gerund or an infinitive may be possible.

```
┌────────────────────────────────────────────────────────────────────────────┐
│ ▢                          I'm in a play! - Message                      ▣▤ │
├────────────────────────────────────────────────────────────────────────────┤
│  Send    Save    Insert File...    Priority ▾    Options...                 │
├────────────────────────────────────────────────────────────────────────────┤
│  ┌──────┐                                                                   │
│  │ To...│  mls1@marksmith.com                                              │
│  ├──────┤                                                                   │
│  │ Cc...│                                                                   │
│  └──────┘                                                                   │
│  Subject: │ I'm in a play!                                                  │
├────────────────────────────────────────────────────────────────────────────┤
```

Dear Uncle Mark,

You know how much I enjoy (act) __acting__ . You always encouraged me (take)
               1 drama classes. And you were the one who persuaded me (try)
_____ for a part in a play. I've worked very hard, and at times I didn't
      3

think I was good at (act) _____ . In fact, there were times I wanted to
             4

stop (act) _____ and do something else with my time. Well, I have
    5

good news! Now I don't regret (spend) _____ so much of my time on
          6

acting. I have a part in the school play!

It's not a big role. I don't come onstage until Act 2. But in one important

scene, I pretend (be) _____ very sick. In another scene, I say an
      7

important line, and then I continue (stand) _____ on stage for about
          8

two minutes. I look forward to (rehearse) _____ the play. I expect
        9

(learn) _____ a lot about the theater from this experience.
    10

I'm not very good at (remember) _____ lines, but I will try
        11

(do) _____ my best and remember them. I hope I remember
   12

(say) _____ all my lines correctly!
   13

Oh, I almost forgot (tell) _____ you . . . I would really like
        14

(invite) _____ you to the opening night of my play. I hope
    15

(see) _____ you there!
   16

Your niece,

Katira

9e Infinitives after Certain Adjectives, Nouns, and Indefinite Pronouns

Student Book p. 268

⊓ Practice

Complete the sentences with the infinitive form of verbs from the list.

borrow	have	run
do	hear	stop
drive	let	tell
find	pick up	visit
go	practice	

Jenna: I passed my driving test and got my license! And I'm proud _to tell_ you

that I got an almost perfect score!

Mother: I'm so pleased _____ that, honey.

Jenna: So can I borrow the car this afternoon? I have some friends

_____.

Mother: I know you're eager _____. But I'm not sure you're ready to

take the car by yourself. I'm hesitant _____ you take the car

on the busy roads. I think it's important for you _____

more first.

Jenna: Please? I'll be careful _____ only on quiet streets. I'm not

likely _____ a lot of traffic on Belmont Street.

Mother: I don't know. I think this weekend is a better time for you

_____ the car. I have some things _____
9   10

this afternoon, and I need the car.

Jenna: Do you have any errands for me _____? I'd be willing
11

_____ at the store for you. I'd be happy _____
12   13

some groceries for dinner tonight.

Mother: I guess that would be all right. Now that I think about it, it will be pretty

convenient for me _____ another licensed driver in the house!
14

12 Practice

Rewrite the sentences using infinitives instead of gerunds.

1. Obeying traffic laws is important.

   It's important to obey traffic laws.

2. Understanding how your car works is necessary.

   _____

3. Failing a driving test is disappointing.

   _____

4. Not having a car is frustrating for some teenagers.

   _____

5. Driving without insurance is illegal.

   _____

6. Not wearing a seatbelt is dangerous.

   _____

7. For young people, getting their driver's license is very exciting.

   _____

8. Owning and maintaining a car can be expensive.

   _____

9. Saving money for a car isn't easy for everyone.

   _____

9f *Too* and *Enough* Followed by Infinitives

Student Book p. 270

13 **Practice**

Jared likes his English class better than his psychology class. Use information from the chart to write three sentences about the classes using *too, enough,* and *not . . . enough.*

	Psychology Class	English Class
1	There are so many people that not everyone has a chair to sit on.	There are plenty of chairs for everyone to sit on.
2	The professor speaks so softly that the students in the back can't hear him.	The professor speaks loudly, and everyone can hear.
3	The professor speaks so quickly that Jared can't take notes.	The professor speaks slowly, and Jared can take notes.
4	The windows are so high that they can't be opened.	The windows are low, and they can be opened.
5	The class is at 8:00 A.M., and the students are so tired that they can't pay attention.	The class is at 10:00 A.M.; the students are awake and can pay attention.
6	The students are so lazy that they don't do the homework.	The students are so motivated that they always do the homework.

1. **a.** *In Jared's psychology class, there are too many people for everyone to have a chair.*

   b. *In his psychology class, there aren't enough chairs for everyone to sit on.*

   c. *In his English class, there are enough chairs for eveyone to sit on.*

2. **a.** The professor in his psychology class _____

   b. In his psychology class, _____

   c. In his English class, _____

3. **a.** The psychology professor _____

   b. The psychology professor _____

   c. The English professor _____

4. **a.** In the psychology classroom, _____

   b. In the psychology classroom, _____

   c. In the English classroom, _____

5. **a.** In the 8:00 A.M. psychology class, _____

   b. In the 8:00 A.M. psychology class, _____

   c. In the 10:00 A.M. English class, _____

6. **a.** The psychology students _____

   b. The psychology students _____

   c. The English students _____

|14| Practice

Complete the sentences with *too, enough, not . . . enough,* or *very*.

1. I can't afford to take a vacation. I don't have _____ money.

2. There is _____ time to review for the test, so we'll do that in class tomorrow.

3. We're _____ tired, but we'll go to your party anyway.

4. I'm sorry we're _____ tired to go to your party, but thanks for inviting us.

5. It's _____ dangerous to ice skate on the pond — don't do it!

6. Are there _____ people to get a group discount?

7. Roberta is _____ smart; she got all A's last semester.

8. You should have the last piece of cake; there is _____ for two people.

9. In the United States, eighteen is old _____ to vote.

10. Some people think that fifteen-year-olds are _____ young to date.

15 Practice

Write five sentences about the photograph. Use *too, enough,* and *not . . . enough* with infinitives.

1. _____
_____

2. _____
_____

3. _____
_____

4. _____
_____

5. _____
_____

9g The Infinitive of Purpose

Student Book p. 273

16 Practice

Rewrite each sentence twice, replacing *for* with the verbs in parentheses. The first time, use an infinitive. The second time, use the more formal *in order to* + a base verb.

1. David went to the library for a book about Spain. (locate)

   a. *David went to the library to locate a book about Spain.*

   b. *David went to the library in order to locate a book about Spain.*

2. David wanted to visit Spain for his relatives there. (see)

   a. _____

   b. _____

3. He studied the book for information about his family's town. (find)

   a. _____

   b. _____

4. He got a summer job for travel money. (earn)

a. _____

b. _____

5. He signed up at the community center for Spanish classes. (take)

a. _____

b. _____

6. He used the Internet for a cheap airplane ticket to Spain. (buy)

a. _____

b. _____

17 Practice

Ellen has moved into a new apartment. What does she need to buy or do? Where must she go to buy or do these things? Write six sentences using *to, for,* and *in order to*.

Example: *She must go to the furniture store to buy furniture.*

1. _____

2. _____

3. _____

4. _____

5. _____

6. _____

18 Practice

What should you do in order not to have problems in school? Rewrite the following sentences using *in order not to* + a verb.

1. You should sit near the front of the class so you won't miss anything the teacher says.

   You should sit near the front of the class in order not to miss anything the teacher says.

2. You should review your notes so you won't forget information.

   _____

3. You should buy file folders so you won't lose your papers.

   _____

4. You should allow plenty of time to get to class so you won't be late.

   _____

5. You should buy a day planner or a PDA so you won't waste time.

   _____

6. You should get enough sleep and exercise so you won't get sick.

   _____

7. You should join student clubs so you won't feel lonely.

   _____

8. You should ask your teachers for help so you won't fall behind.

   _____

9. (*your own advice*)

   _____

10. (*your own advice*)

    _____

Perfect Infinitives and Perfect Gerunds;
Passive Voice of Infinitives and Gerunds
Student Book p. 275

19 **Practice**
**Read why Jim was late for work. Complete the sentences using the perfect infinitive
or perfect gerund form of the verbs in parentheses. Some sentences require the active
voice (*to have* + past participle or *having* + past participle). Others require the
passive voice (*to have been* + past participle or *having been* + past participle).**

I had such a terrible morning! After (wake up) *having woken up* an hour late,
                                                            1
I couldn't find my car keys anywhere. Then I remembered that I had put them in my brown

pants, which I had taken to be cleaned yesterday. (warn) _____
                                                                        2
not to come late to work again, I knew there was no time to waste. I ran down the street

to the bus stop. I thought I was really smart (remember) _____
                                                                        3
the 8:30 bus. But I couldn't figure out why no one else was at the bus stop. Then I looked at

the schedule. The schedule had changed, and the bus now came at 8:20. I was angry with

myself for (not, look) _____ at the schedule before (leave)
                                  4

_____ my house. After (miss) _____
              5   6
the bus, I decided my only option was to run to work. Then, after (run)

_____ two miles to the office, I sat down at my desk. I wasn't
              7
happy (arrive) _____ fifteen minutes late. But I thought I was
                              8
really lucky (not, notice) _____ by the boss. I expected (call)
                                          9
_____ into his office before I even sat down. Then I heard that
              10
the boss, (take) _____ the day off, isn't even here today!
                          11

Practice

Rewrite each sentence about the photo twice, using *need* + a gerund and *need* + a passive infinitive (*to be* + past participle). Use the verbs in parentheses.

1. There are too many papers on Barbara's desk. (file)

    a. *The papers need filing.*

    b. *The papers need to be filed.*

2. There are 28 voicemail messages on her phone. (delete)

    a. _____

    b. _____

3. Three meetings must be set up before 4:00. (schedule)

    a. _____

    b. _____

4. The computer is down. (service)

    a. _____

    b. _____

5. The copy machine is broken. (repair)

    a. _____

    b. _____

6. Her assistant quit this morning. (replace)

    a. _____

    b. _____

Gerunds and Base Verbs with Verbs of Perception

Student Book p. 279

21 Practice

Read the following police report. Decide if the events describe a single complete action or an action in progress. If it is a single complete action, circle the base verb form. If it is an action in progress, circle the gerund form.

Police Report

At 6:00 P.M. in Shoreline Park, a 25-year-old woman named Ji Lee witnessed a crime. She was reading a book when she heard something (move / **moving**) in the bushes behind her. She turned around and saw a
1
man in the process of (crawl / crawling) towards an elderly woman who was
2
sitting at a park bench. The older woman did not seem to notice the man (come / coming) towards her. Ji watched the man (walk / walking) to the
3   **4**
end of the path and (stopping / stop) just behind the woman's purse. She
5
realized she was observing a crime (happen / happening) before her eyes!
6
She didn't want the thief to turn around and see her
(watch / watching) him, so she moved behind a tree. Earlier, she had seen
7
the man (put / putting) his hand in his pocket as he approached the bench,
8
and she thought he might have a weapon! She observed the man's hand
(reach / reaching) down into the woman's purse. Ji shouted, "Help!", but
9
there was no one around to hear her (shout / shouting). Fortunately, she
10
surprised the man. She watched the man quickly (remove / removing) his
11
hand from the woman's bag and then (run / running) away. Having seen a
12
crime (be / being) committed in this park, Ji isn't eager to return to it
13
anytime soon.

9j ◈ Person + Gerund

Student Book p. 281

22 **Practice**

Rewrite the sentences with a person + a gerund. Give answers in both informal and formal English.

1. My friend Beth talks on her cell phone when we go out for coffee. I don't like it.

   a. *I don't like Beth talking on her cell phone when we go out for coffee.*

   b. *I don't like Beth's talking on her cell phone when we go out for coffee.*

2. Her friends call and interrupt our conversation. I can't stand it.

   a. _____

   b. _____

3. They don't ask her if she's free to talk on the phone. I don't approve of that.

   a. _____

   b. _____

4. My boyfriend turns his phone off in restaurants. I appreciate that.

   a. _____

   b. _____

168

Unit 9

5. He doesn't want to hear the phone ring in public places. I respect that.

a. _____

b. _____

6. On the other hand, sometimes my boyfriend doesn't answer the phone when I call. I'm annoyed by that.

a. _____

b. _____

7. Beth ignores me when her friends call. I'm tired of it.

a. _____

b. _____

8. I politely ask her to get off the phone. She doesn't hear me.

a. _____

b. _____

23 Practice

Read the sentences. Write *C* next to the sentence if the "person + gerund" pattern is used correctly. Write *I* if it is used incorrectly.

_____ **1.** My sister and I have never been close, so I was surprised at asking me to be the maid of honor in her wedding.

_____ **2.** Chris loves to listen to the symphony. He especially enjoys they playing free concerts in the park.

_____ **3.** Janet was tired of her friends' criticizing her clothing style.

_____ **4.** Rick's parents didn't hear his getting in late.

_____ **5.** The instructor couldn't stand the students talking in class.

_____ **6.** Her friends laugh at her singing.

_____ **7.** We were encouraged by the governor supports education.

_____ **8.** Do you mind them clean the house while you are working?

A **Choose the best answer, A, B, C, or D, to complete the sentence. Mark your answer by darkening the oval with the same letter.**

1. I don't remember _____ to Europe when I was two years old.

   A. to go   Ⓐ Ⓑ Ⓒ Ⓓ
   B. going
   C. for to go
   D. for going

2. The new employee isn't capable _____ doing the job.

   A. in   Ⓐ Ⓑ Ⓒ Ⓓ
   B. to
   C. of
   D. about

3. Some people cut up their credit cards in order _____ them.

   A. not to use   Ⓐ Ⓑ Ⓒ Ⓓ
   B. for not to use
   C. to use
   D. not use

4. The teacher is always willing _____ students with their assignments.

   A. for to help   Ⓐ Ⓑ Ⓒ Ⓓ
   B. helping
   C. help
   D. to help

5. The coach didn't _____ five games in a row.

   A. expect us win   Ⓐ Ⓑ Ⓒ Ⓓ
   B. expect to us win
   C. expect win
   D. expect us to win

6. Stella wanted _____ the assignment by lunchtime because she expected _____ to present her work to the class that afternoon.

   A. to have been   Ⓐ Ⓑ Ⓒ Ⓓ
   finished / being asked
   B. to have finished / to be asked
   C. to have been finishing / to be asked
   D. to finish / having been asked

7. I was pleased at _____ good grades.

   A. to have earned   Ⓐ Ⓑ Ⓒ Ⓓ
   B. having earned
   C. earning
   D. had earned

8. We regret _____ you that we cannot offer you the job at this time.

   A. to inform   Ⓐ Ⓑ Ⓒ Ⓓ
   B. informing
   C. for informing
   D. informed

9. Francie resented _____ to the event at the last minute.

   A. to have been invited   Ⓐ Ⓑ Ⓒ Ⓓ
   B. having invited
   C. having been invited
   D. to have invited

10. The girls are _____ to go to the rock concert alone; it's not safe.

   A. too young   Ⓐ Ⓑ Ⓒ Ⓓ
   B. young enough
   C. not young enough
   D. young

B **Find the underlined word or phrase, A, B, C, or D, that is incorrect. Mark your answer by darkening the oval with the same letter.**

1. I used to enjoy <u>going</u> <u>running</u>, but I
   A B
   <u>stopped to run</u> after I <u>injured</u> my knee.
   C D

   Ⓐ Ⓑ Ⓒ Ⓓ

2. What would <u>stop</u> the world champion <u>for</u>
   A B
   <u>winning</u> the Boston Marathon <u>next week</u>?
   C D

   Ⓐ Ⓑ Ⓒ Ⓓ

3. When Emily <u>refused</u> <u>to clean her room</u>,
   A B
   her parents <u>wouldn't</u> <u>allow to watch</u> TV.
   C D

   Ⓐ Ⓑ Ⓒ Ⓓ

4. If you have <u>some time</u> <u>for to discuss</u> the
   A B
   proposal, I'm <u>eager to talk</u> about it
   C
   <u>with you</u>.
   D

   Ⓐ Ⓑ Ⓒ Ⓓ

5. He <u>doesn't need</u> <u>making</u> a lot of money,
   A B
   but he <u>would like</u> <u>to have</u> a fun job.
   C D

   Ⓐ Ⓑ Ⓒ Ⓓ

6. If you're <u>taking</u> a long trip, <u>don't forget</u>
   A B
   <u>checking</u> the oil in your car <u>before you go</u>.
   C D

   Ⓐ Ⓑ Ⓒ Ⓓ

7. My sister <u>was</u> thrilled <u>to have been</u> <u>chose</u>
   A B C
   <u>to represent</u> the company at the
   D
   conference last season.

   Ⓐ Ⓑ Ⓒ Ⓓ

8. <u>For to purchase</u> this ticket, <u>it's necessary</u>
   A B
   <u>to show</u> <u>your identification</u> at the counter.
   C D

   Ⓐ Ⓑ Ⓒ Ⓓ

9. The family <u>was happy</u> <u>to have</u> <u>found</u> their
   A B C
   lost dog after <u>searched</u> for many weeks.
   D

   Ⓐ Ⓑ Ⓒ Ⓓ

10. <u>Having argued</u> with the neighbors, I was
    A
    <u>surprised</u> at <u>they</u> <u>bringing</u> us a nice gift.
    B C D

    Ⓐ Ⓑ Ⓒ Ⓓ

Gerunds and Infinitives

UNIT 10 AGREEMENT AND PARALLEL STRUCTURE

10a Subject-Verb Agreement: General Rules Part 1

Student Book p. 292

☐ 1 Practice

Complete the sentences by circling the correct form of the verbs in parentheses.

Sports Unlimited Fitness Center

Greetings, members! This month we would like to inform you about new classes and facilities at our gym. You will find that many changes (has /(have)) been made.
1

First of all, the new building (is / are) finished. This news (is / are) good for tennis
2 **3**
players: the building (contain / contains) two tennis courts! Playing basketball (is / are)
4 **5**
also something that members can enjoy in the new building. Two courts (has / have) been
6
built in the back of this building.

The women's locker room (has / have) been moved to the new building as well. New
7
showers, a Jacuzzi, and a sauna (were / was) installed there last week. The men's lockers
8
and sauna (is / are) still located in the old building. However, plans to remodel the men's
9
locker room next year (is / are) currently being discussed.
10
All members (is / are) required to get a new ID card. Electronics (is / are) changing
11 **12**
our ID card system. Scanning a bar code (replace / replaces) the old paper card system.
13
Susan and Joe (has / have) the new plastic cards for you at the front desk. Until the end
14

of this month, either the old cards or the new cards (work / works).
15
After this month, however, all the old cards (stop / stops) working.
16
Step aerobics (is / are) now a class offered at our gym! Step
17
classes (is / are) held Monday through Friday at 6:00 A.M. and
18
6:00 P.M. Tuesday and Thursday (is / are) the most popular days for
19

these classes, so be sure to sign up in advance. If you're looking for a spinning class,

Monday morning or Wednesday evening (is / are) the best time to go. If you've never
                                          20

tried spinning, all of our instructors (is / are) happy to schedule a thirty-minute
                                       21

private lesson and (show / shows) you how to use the bike.
                  22

2 | Practice

Think of a group such as a class, a school, a gym, a sports team, or a club. Write sentences about this group. Explain what people do or have to do. Use the simple present or the present perfect and the quantity words.

Example: *I belong to a chorus. All members come to practice every day at 4:00.*
Most people in the group have been singing for a long time. Everyone loves to perform at the concerts. Not everyone has taken private singing lessons. . .

1. All _____ .

2. Most _____ .

3. Some _____ .

4. Each _____ .

5. Every _____ .

6. Everyone _____ .

7. Not everyone _____ .

8. Any _____ .

9. Almost all _____ .

10b Subject-Verb Agreement: General Rules Part 2

Student Book p. 295

3 | **Practice**

Complete the sentences with a singular or plural form of *be*. Pay attention to time words; use present and past tenses when necessary.

There ____*is*____ good news for our
1

soccer team these days. Yesterday's game, despite

concerns about the weather, _____ a
2

major victory: the Cobras _____ now
3

headed to the community league playoffs!

Co-captain Dennis Garcia, along with Co-cap-

tain Beth Carlson, _____ very excited
4

about this next step. Garcia explains, "Going to the

playoffs, which will take place next week,

_____ the highest honor this team
5

could hope for. We've faced a lot of challenges this season. But those lost games, together

with the lost hopes, _____ now far behind us. We _____ a
6   7

championship team!"

Carlson adds, "Bad weather, as well as the loss of some players, _____
8

something that every team has to face at some point. But there were a lot of concerns

back in the beginning of the season. There _____ many new players who joined
9

our team, and there _____ more injured players than we've had in the past.
10

There _____ also a new coach who joined our team halfway through the
11

season. Whenever a team goes through that amount of change, there _____
12

always going to be some confusion. There _____ certainly going to be lost
13

matches and lost hopes while the team works to redefine itself."

Rich Regan, the new coach, _____ perhaps more excited than any of his
                                    14
players. "The Cobras, even with this year's losses, _____ showing great
                                                         15
improvement from previous years," says Coach Regan. "And the great thing about my
coming into the season halfway through _____ the chance to bring in new
                                              16
energy and fresh hopes."

This year the Cobras, minus the five players who have left the team,

_____ fighting back with their new coach and new, talented players. Regan,
       17
Garcia, and Carlson _____ all optimistic that the chances of winning the
                           18
playoffs _____ very high. The group of new players _____ beginning
              19   20
to show great talent. One of the new players, Isabella Cherrez, _____ especially
                                                                      21
worth watching, according to Coach Regan.

Unfortunately, rain, along with high winds, _____ predicted for Saturday's
                                                  22
match. But the players, together with their captains and coach, _____ not likely
                                                                      23
to have their spirits dampened. This _____ a team with a winning spirit, and
                                           24
there _____ no doubt that they will fight hard to win this important match.
           25

4 | Practice

**Describe the photographs. Complete the sentences with your own ideas. Use *be* or
other verbs in the simple present or present progressive. Make sure that subjects
and verbs agree.**

A.

1. All of these people _____*are trying to fit*_____
   _____*into the doorway.*_____

2. One of these people _____
   _____

3. All of these people _____
   _____

4. Almost all of these people _____
   _____

5. Half of these people _____
   _____

B.

1. All four of these boys _____

   _____

2. Two of the boys _____

   _____

3. The small boy in the striped shirt _____

   _____

4. One of the older boys _____

   _____

5. The challenge for three of the boys _____

   _____

C.

1. The little girl together with her parents

   _____

   _____

2. Everyone in this family _____

   _____

3. The parents of the little girl _____

4. The exciting thing for her parents _____

10c Subject-Verb Agreement with Quantity Words

Student Book p. 297

5 Practice

Complete the sentences with the correct form of the verbs in parentheses. Note that these sentences talk about people, not time, money, distance, or weight.

1. Some of the facts about this year's graduating class (be) _____ *are* _____ fascinating.

2. Two-thirds of the graduating seniors (plan) _____ to attend a four-year college or a community college.

3. Almost half of them (want) _____ to attend graduate school someday.

4. Over half of the seniors (have) _____ been accepted into a four-year college for the fall.

5. Most of our school's graduates (attend) _____ the state university.

6. The number of students accepted into the state university (increase) _____ every year.

7. A number of seniors (work) _____ part-time while attending school.

8. Some of the students (have) _____ job offers already.

9. Five percent of the graduating class (have) _____ won national honors.

10. One of the seniors (be) _____ the recipient of a four-year scholarship to Yale University.

11. Some of the graduation ceremony (be) _____ reserved to honor award-winning students.

12. Every one of the students (make) _____ his or her teacher proud!

13. None of the students (miss) _____ graduation day.

14. Four years (be) _____ a long time to work on earning a diploma.

6 Practice

Read the sentences. Write C next to the sentence if the subject and verb used with the quantity word agree and the sentence is correct. Write I if they do not agree and the sentence is incorrect.

_____ 1. Five minutes is all the time I have to speak with you.

_____ 2. Some of the flowers has died.

_____ 3. A number of people suffers from migraine headaches.

_____ 4. None of the critics likes the new movie.

_____ 5. Five hours are not enough sleep for most people.

_____ 6. You can borrow any of my books, but some of them belong to the library.

_____ 7. One of the lamps in the living room are broken.

_____ 8. Our state is very dry this summer, and two inches of rain aren't going to be enough to solve the problem.

_____ 9. Two-thirds of people under twenty-five do not have health insurance.

_____ 10. The number of crimes committed last year are frightening.

10d Parallel Structure

Student Book p. 301

7 Practice

Underline the parallel structure in the following sentences. Then write which grammatical form (nouns, adjectives, verbs, adverbs, gerunds, or infinitives) the parallel structures contain.

1. Domino tiles are <u>thick</u> and <u>heavy</u> enough to stand on edge.   _adjectives_

2. Dominoes is a very popular game in South America, Asia, and North America.   _____

3. Learning how to play dominoes is easy, but winning dominoes requires strategy.   _____

4. If you look at a domino with many dots and a domino with fewer dots, the "heavier" domino is the one with more dots.   _____

5. To begin playing dominoes, place the tiles face down on a table and shuffle them by hand.   _____

6. Players take turns placing tiles on the table, matching the number of dots to those already laid down, and decreasing their amount of tiles. _____

7. The object of the game might be to play all of one's tiles, or to have the highest score at the end of the game. _____

8. There are two main types of domino games: block games and draw games. _____

9. In a block game, if players can't play and eliminate any of their tiles, they lose their turn. _____

10. In a draw game, players take new tiles from the common pile and don't stop until they get one they can play. _____

11. Dominoes is an exciting and strategic game that can be enjoyed by people of all ages. _____

12. Many serious dominoes players compete in regional, national, and international tournaments. _____

8 Practice

Correct the errors in parallel structure. Then write which grammatical form (nouns, adjectives, verbs, adverbs, gerunds, or infinitives) the parallel structures contain. Some sentences have no errors.

1. Backgammon, a game for two players, requires a backgammon set, two sets of dice, and ~~you need~~ thirty checkers. _____nouns_____

2. The backgammon board has twenty-four triangles, which lie in four quadrants and alternating in color. _____

3. A bar down the center of the board separates the players' "home board" and "outer board." _____

4. The objects of the game are to move all of your checkers around the board, to bring them to your own home board, and taking them off the board. _____

5. The first player to move all of his or her checkers and to

take them off the board wins the game. _____

6. Players must roll the dice again if a die fallen outside the

board, hits a checker, or does not land flat. _____

7. If a player's move is unfinished or illegality, the opponent

is allowed to accept that move. _____

9 | Practice

Answer the following questions with information about yourself. Use parallel structure and correct punctuation.

1. What are (or were) your three favorite subjects in school?

My favorite subjects in school are chemistry, math, and art.

2. What three adjectives best describe you?

_____

3. What are two things that you do every morning?

_____

4. What three chores around the house do you dislike doing?

_____

5. What are three things that you want to do in the future?

_____

6. What are two things that you don't want to do in the future?

_____

7. In your opinion, what three activities are the most useful for relieving stress?

_____

8. In your opinion, what are the two biggest causes of stress among people your age?

_____

9. What are two words that describe how you speak English?

_____

10. What are three things that someone should do or see if they visit your city?

_____

10 Practice

Write a paragraph about a game that you know. Explain what materials you need and how to play the game. Check your sentences for parallel structure and correct punctuation.

_____

_____

_____

_____

_____

_____

_____

10e Coordinating Conjunctions

Student Book p. 304

11 Practice

Combine each pair of sentences into one longer sentence using a coordinating conjunction. Use correct punctuation.

1. Alicia wants to buy fruit. She doesn't know what kind.

   Alicia wants to buy fruit,

   but she doesn't know what kind.

2. The grapefruit looks ripe. The plums look very fresh.

   _____

   _____

3. Apples are on sale today. She should buy a lot of them.

   _____

   _____

4. She could use fresh fruit in a dessert. She could use it in a salad instead.

   _____

5. The strawberries look delicious. They are too expensive.

   _____

6. She should shop at the farmer's market. The prices are lower. The fruit is fresher.

_____

7. Alicia would like to make an apple pie. She doesn't know how.

_____

8. If she wants to bake a pie, she should buy a baking dish. She doesn't have one.

_____

12 Practice

Write a paragraph of at least six sentences describing this house. Use each coordinating conjunction (_and, for, or, so, but, yet_) at least once. Use correct punctuation.

_____

_____

_____

_____

_____

13 Practice

Read the sentences for errors with conjunctions or with commas. If the sentence is correct, write _C_. If the sentence is incorrect, write _I_ and correct the error(s).

_____ **1.** My sister was always good at math, so I was always better at English.

_____ **2.** Jacob applied for six jobs, for he didn't get any of them.

_____ **3.** We were very tired, but we stayed up and studied anyway.

_____ **4.** The actor was seventy years old yet he was still very handsome.

_____ **5.** You can leave a voicemail message or you can call back later.

_____ **6.** They tried to take notes, and they couldn't hear the teacher.

_____ **7.** Drew's parents are coming to visit, and they are bringing lots of food for him.

_____ **8.** The movie was so bad that we wanted to leave, or we stayed and watched until the end.

10f Correlative Conjunctions: *Both . . . And; Not Only . . . But Also; Either . . . Or; Neither . . . Nor*
Student Book p. 307

| 14 | Practice

Read the sentences about twin brothers. Circle the correct form of the verbs in parentheses.

1. Both Brandon and Roger (is / are) seniors at Garfield High School.

2. Both Brandon and his brother (plan / plans) to attend college.

3. Neither the twins nor their parents (want / wants) a college that is far from home.

4. Both Brandon and Roger (prefers/ prefer) to go to the same college.

5. Either the University of Michigan or Michigan State (are / is) a good choice for the brothers.

6. Not only Roger's teachers but also Roger (think / thinks) that Michigan State will accept him.

7. Either business or economics (interest / interests) Brandon.

8. Neither mathematics nor political science (interest / interests) Roger.

9. Not only the University of Michigan but also Michigan State (offer / offers) basketball scholarships.

10. Either a grant or student loans (is / are) going to be useful for paying for college, since both boys will be studying at the same time.

Practice

Combine each pair of sentences into one longer sentence. Use the correlative conjunctions in parentheses.

1. Roger plays basketball. Brandon plays basketball. (both / and)

   Both Roger and Brandon play basketball.

2. Roger plays basketball. Brandon plays basketball. (not only / but also)

   _____

3. Roger does not like math. Brandon does not like math. (neither / nor)

   _____

4. Roger does not enjoy math. He does not enjoy history. (neither / nor)

   _____

5. Roger does not enjoy math. He does not enjoy history. (either / or)

   _____

6. Brandon works on the weekends or he goes out with his friends. (either / or)

   _____

7. Brandon likes fixing cars or repairing electronic equipment for fun. (either / or)

   _____

8. The twins like spending time with each other. Their parents like spending time with each other. (both / and)

   _____

   _____

9. Roger's mother wants the boys to choose a college close to home. Roger's father wants the boys to choose a college close to home. (not only / but also)

   _____

   _____

10. Roger's mother wants the boys to visit often. She wants her sons to be independent. (not only / but also)

   _____

   _____

16 Practice

Write sentences about each pair of jobs. Use correlative conjunctions and your own ideas.

Example: *Both veterinarians and medical doctors need to study medicine. Not only medical doctors but also veterinarians want to help others get well.*

A.

Veterinarian (Vet)

Medical Doctor

1. both / and

_____

2. not only / but also

_____

3. neither / nor

_____

4. either / or

_____

B.

Chef

Waiter

1. both / and

_____

2. not only / but also

_____

3. neither / nor

_____

4. either / or

_____

C. Think of two other jobs and compare them using correlative conjunctions in your own sentences.

Job 1: _____ Job 2: _____

1. both / and

_____

2. not only / but also

_____

3. neither / nor

_____

4. either / or

_____

SELF-TEST

A **Choose the best answer, A, B, C, or D, to complete the sentence. Mark your answer by darkening the oval with the same letter.**

1. I've always enjoyed seeing my family and
   _____.

   A. to talk about   Ⓐ Ⓑ Ⓒ Ⓓ
   old times
   B. talking about old times
   C. talked about old times
   D. talk about old times

2. My friend hopes to attend either _____
   next fall.

   A. Seattle University or   Ⓐ Ⓑ Ⓒ Ⓓ
   Pacific University
   B. Seattle University nor Pacific University
   C. Seattle University and Pacific University
   D. to Seattle University and to Pacific
   University

3. The instructor never arrived, _____ the
   students went home.

   A. but   Ⓐ Ⓑ Ⓒ Ⓓ
   B. so
   C. or
   D. for

4. Jane's mother will _____.

   A. buy her neither a car   Ⓐ Ⓑ Ⓒ Ⓓ
   nor lend her one
   B. not neither buy her a
   car nor lend her one
   C. buy her a car nor lend her one
   D. neither buy her a car nor lend her one

5. Neither Greg _____ happy with the test
   results.

   A. or his teachers are   Ⓐ Ⓑ Ⓒ Ⓓ
   B. or his teachers is
   C. nor his teachers are
   D. nor his teachers is

6. The doctor told him to exercise, _____
   he didn't take the doctor's advice.

   A. but   Ⓐ Ⓑ Ⓒ Ⓓ
   B. for
   C. or
   D. so

7. Many people dislike New England's
   summers because of the _____.

   A. hot and humidity   Ⓐ Ⓑ Ⓒ Ⓓ
   B. heat and humidity
   C. heat and humid
   D. hot and humid

8. The car makes not only a loud noise
   _____.

   A. but a bad smell also   Ⓐ Ⓑ Ⓒ Ⓓ
   B. also a bad smell
   C. but also a bad smell
   D. but also makes a bad smell

9. If you feel _____, you should call a
   doctor.

   A. pain, tired, and thirsty   Ⓐ Ⓑ Ⓒ Ⓓ
   B. pain, tired, and thirst
   C. pain, tiredness, and thirsty
   D. pain, tiredness, and thirst

10. The computer _____.

    A. both has a flat screen   Ⓐ Ⓑ Ⓒ Ⓓ
    and new speakers
    B. both have a flat screen
    and new speakers
    C. has both a flat screen
    and new speakers
    D. a flat screen and new speakers both

Agreement and Parallel Structure

B **Find the underlined word or phrase, A, B, C, or D, that is incorrect. Mark your answer by darkening the oval with the same letter.**

1. Thirty minutes <u>are</u> <u>not enough time</u> for
          A   B

   some students <u>to take</u> the test and
             C

   <u>to do well</u>.
     D

   (A) (B) (C) (D)

2. The <u>instructions</u> <u>for building the</u>
        A   B

   <u>patio table</u> <u>is</u> difficult <u>to understand</u>.
      C   D

   (A) (B) (C) (D)

3. <u>Each</u> of the presidential candidates
     A

   <u>promise</u> <u>to lower taxes</u> and <u>to spend</u> more
     B   C   D

   money on education.

   (A) (B) (C) (D)

4. Economics <u>don't</u> usually <u>interest me</u>, <u>but</u>
           A   B   C

   my economics class <u>is</u> really exciting.
                  D

   (A) (B) (C) (D)

5. <u>There is</u> many reasons why mathematics
      A

   <u>is useful</u> not only in school <u>but also</u>
      B   C

   <u>for work</u>.
     D

   (A) (B) (C) (D)

6. <u>The number of</u> traffic accidents <u>caused by</u>
        A   B

   cell phones <u>are</u> <u>increasing</u> every year.
            C   D

   (A) (B) (C) (D)

7. <u>Falling in love</u> can make people <u>feel</u>
       A   B

   <u>happiness</u>, tired, and <u>worried</u> all at once.
     C   D

   (A) (B) (C) (D)

8. <u>There is</u> <u>a lot of traffic</u> at this time of
      A   B

   day, <u>for</u> we should wait an hour until the
        C

   roads <u>are</u> less busy.
         D

   (A) (B) (C) (D)

9. Either the ocean <u>or</u> the mountains <u>is</u> a
               A   B

   good place to go <u>for</u> a vacation, <u>but</u> the
              C   D

   choice is yours.

   (A) (B) (C) (D)

10. Ed was feeling tired all the time, <u>so</u> the
                          A

    doctor recommended <u>both</u> <u>exercising more</u>
                   B   C

    and <u>to take</u> vitamins.
        D

    (A) (B) (C) (D)

UNIT 11 NOUN CLAUSES AND REPORTED SPEECH

11a Noun Clauses Beginning with *That*

Student Book p. 318

1 Practice

Read the sentences. Write *C* next to the sentence if the *that* noun clause is correct. Write *I* if it is incorrect.

_____ 1. That you don't know what you're doing is clear.

_____ 2. We believe your work is not up to standard.

_____ 3. I don't hope so.

_____ 4. I hope not.

_____ 5. He's a manager doesn't change things.

_____ 6. They think so.

_____ 7. We think so.

_____ 8. You thought so that he was here.

_____ 9. It's not surprising that he was fired.

_____ 10. We can't prove not that the intern stole the money.

2 Practice

Read about Christopher Columbus. Underline the noun clauses. Some begin with *that* and others have *that* omitted.

Christopher Columbus, originally from Genoa, Italy, was an explorer who knew the world was round. He predicted he could find a trade route to Asia by sailing west. He had a very difficult time raising money for his voyage, so he finally appealed to Queen Isabella and King Ferdinand of Spain. They decided that Columbus might be right, and it would be in the best interest of Spain to find out. Columbus set out to prove that he was right.

On his first voyage in 1492, he arrived in the Bahamas and established a settlement there, but he thought he had arrived in Asia, and when he went back to Spain, he told the king and queen that he had. Many people doubted that this was true. On his second trip, Columbus discovered his original settlement had been destroyed, and he had to spend most of his time governing instead of exploring. He was an unfit governor, and although he made a total of four trips to the New World, he died regretting he had never found the route to Asia that he was convinced existed.

3 | Practice

Write negative responses using the verbs in parentheses and *so* or *not*.

1. Boss: Can you stay late tonight?

   Kevin: I (be afraid) <u>'m afraid not</u>. My wife is working tonight, so I have to pick up the kids.

2. Kevin: Sean, are you working late tonight?

   Sean: I (hope) _____.

3. Sean: Do you have any printer paper?

   Jackie: I (think) _____, but I'll look.

4. Jackie: Are you leaving now? It's 5:00.

   Sean: I (guess) _____ because I have to finish this before tomorrow.

5. Sean: Do you have a little money I could borrow? I'll pay you back tomorrow.

   Jackie: I (believe) _____. I went shopping at lunch, and I think I spent all my cash.

Now respond to the following statements using *think, believe, be afraid, guess,* or *hope*. Use *so* or *not* where appropriate. Explain your answer.

6. The polar ice caps will stop melting.

   _____.

7. Women will receive the same salary as men in the next ten years.

   _____.

8. The spread of AIDS in Africa will stop.

_____ .

9. Movie theaters will disappear.

_____ .

10. Everyone should have cosmetic surgery if they want it.

_____ .

4   Practice

Read about Matt and his family. Then complete the sentences using the prompts.

My brother, Matt, his wife, and his son used to live in the Virgin Islands. In the late summer and fall, the island they lived on was threatened by hurricanes. One year, they knew that a hurricane was coming, so they made as many preparations as possible and sat back and waited for it to come. Late in the night, Matt was woken up when his cat, Sasha, stood on his chest and meowed very loudly in Matt's ear. Finally, Matt woke up and knew something was wrong. The sound of rain was different—louder. Matt got up and went up to check the attic. What he saw shocked him. Most of the roof had been torn away by the wind. As he stood there, more of the roof disappeared into the sky. Matt knew that if they stayed, the house would collapse on top of them. Matt quickly woke up the family, grabbed Sasha, and went to a neighbor's house. The next day, they looked at what was left of their home. If Sasha hadn't woken Matt up, his family could have been seriously injured.

1. Matt thought _that he'd made his house safe_____ .

2. Sasha knew _____ .

3. Matt discovered _____ .

4. He observed _____ .

5. He realized _____ .

6. He decided _____ .

7. Matt and his family believe _____ .

5 | Practice

Complete the sentences.

1. Nostradamus predicted (that) _____ .

2. Ancient Egyptians believed (that) _____ .

3. Galileo observed (that) _____ .

4. Sigmund Freud thought (that) _____ .

5. Hackers show (that) _____ .

6. Actors dream (that) _____ .

7. Babies learn (that) _____ .

8. Everyone knows (that) _____ .

9. As I've grown older, I've noticed (that) _____ .

10. The people of my country think (that) _____ .

11b Noun Clauses Beginning with Wh- Words (Indirect Wh- Questions)

Student Book p. 321

6 | Practice

Read the sentences. Write _C_ next to the sentence if the noun clause beginning with a wh- word (indirect wh- question) is correct. Write _I_ if it is incorrect.

_____ **1.** Do you know where is Kevin?

_____ **2.** Do you know where Kevin is?

_____ **3.** I don't know what is his name.

_____ **4.** I don't know what his name is.

_____ **5.** We're not sure what he does for a living.

_____ **6.** We're not sure what does he do for a living.

_____ **7.** Could you tell me where is the restroom?

_____ **8.** Could you tell me where the restroom is?

_____ **9.** Her parents wanted to know what her plans are.

_____ **10.** Her parents wanted to know what are her plans.

_____ **11.** Did you hear what did she say?

_____ **12.** Did you hear what she said?

7 Practice

Before you get a pet, you should ask yourself questions to be sure that you can care for your new family member. Write indirect wh- questions using "I know."

1. How should I take care of him?

I know how I should take care of him.

2. What does he eat?

_____.

3. When does he sleep?

_____.

4. What kind of toys does he like?

_____.

5. When should I take him to the vet?

_____.

6. What other equipment do I need?

_____.

7. When should I feed him?

_____.

8. How long will he live?

_____.

9. What else should I know?

_____.

Noun Clauses and Reported Speech

8 Practice

Write direct questions from the indirect wh- questions.

1. I didn't hear what she said.

   What did she say? _____

2. I'm not sure when we're supposed to be there.

   _____?

3. She didn't tell me what we should bring.

   _____?

4. Did she tell you when the party starts?

   _____?

5. Do you know who she invited?

   _____?

6. Do you know where she lives?

   _____?

7. Does anyone know how we can get there from here?

   _____?

9 Practice

Read the situations. Write indirect wh- questions using the hints or your own ideas.

A. Your son just got engaged to a woman you don't know. Write indirect questions about her starting with "Your mother/father and I would like to know ...."

education	job
family	time for us to meet her
hometown	where you met

1. Your mother/father and I would like to know _where you met her_____.

2. _____.

3. _____.

4. _____.

5. _____.

6. _____.

B. You're on a tour, but you signed up at the last minute and have a lot of questions for the tour operator. Write indirect questions with "Could you tell me...."

activities	local architecture
cities to visit	meal times
historical sites	shopping opportunities

1. Could you tell me *where we'll be able to do a little shopping?*

2. _____?

3. _____?

4. _____?

5. _____?

6. _____?

C. Your office is relocating. Ask your boss these indirect questions with "Do you know...." and your own ideas.

how long	where
what	why
when	

1. Do you know *what we should do with our files during the move?*

2. _____?

3. _____?

4. _____?

5. _____?

6. _____?

D. A police officer is interviewing a suspect in a robbery case that happened last night at 9:00. Write indirect questions with "Tell us..." and your own ideas.

how	where
what	who with

1. Tell us *where you were last night at 9:00.*

2. _____.

3. _____.

4. _____.

5. _____.

11c Noun Clauses Beginning with *If* or *Whether* (Indirect Yes/No Questions)

Student Book p. 324

10 Practice

Read the sentences. Write *C* next to the sentence if the *if* or *whether* noun clause (indirect yes/no question) is correct. Write *I* if it is incorrect.

_____ **1.** I asked him if he takes the same bus every day.

_____ **2.** I asked him does he take the same bus every day.

_____ **3.** My cousin wanted to know if or not you could come, too.

_____ **4.** My cousin wanted to know whether or not you could come, too.

_____ **5.** She wants to know can she borrow the car.

_____ **6.** She wants to know if she can borrow the car.

_____ **7.** The authorities didn't say if they found the missing woman.

_____ **8.** The authorities didn't say whether they found the missing woman.

11 Practice

You want to plant a garden, and so you want to get information from people at the nursery. Write indirect questions using *if* or *whether* and "Could you tell me," "Do you know," or "I want to know."

1. Does this plant need a lot of light?

I want to know if this plant needs a lot of light.

2. Should I water these plants every day?

_____

3. Do I need to prune these plants often?

_____

4. Do I plant these in the spring or fall?

_____

5. Will they grow in containers?

_____

6. Will they attract butterflies?

_____

7. Do these plants need a lot of care?

_____

8. Should I fertilize them every week?

_____

9. Will they come back next year?

_____

12 Practice

Write direct questions from the indirect yes/no questions.

Marianne lives with two roommates, Sheryl and Kathy. Kathy is in Hawaii on vacation, and Sheryl is talking to her on the phone. Marianne is asking questions for Sheryl to ask Kathy.

1. Marianne: _Is she having a good time_?_____

     Sheryl: Marianne wants to know if you're having a good time.

2. Marianne: _____?

     Sheryl: Now she wants to know if you've met any cute guys.

3. Marianne: _____?

     Sheryl: Marianne has just asked me whether or not you've been to Waikiki yet.

4. Marianne: _____?

     Sheryl: Now she's just asked me if you're coming back soon.

5. Marianne: _____?

     Sheryl: She's wondering if you've tried surfing or not.

6. Marianne: _____?

     Sheryl: Now she wants to know if you've bought us any souvenirs.

13 Practice

Complete the indirect yes/no questions with your own ideas.

1. I've often wondered if I _____ .

2. I recently asked myself whether I _____ .

3. I'm not sure if I could _____ or not.

4. I can't remember if I _____ or not.

5. I don't know if _____ .

11d Quoted Speech

Student Book p. 327

14 Practice

Read the conversation between Lisa and Karl. Write _Q_ next to the sentence if the statement is quoted speech. Write _R_ if it is reported speech.

_____ 1. "What's the weather like there?" Lisa asked.

_____ 2. Karl told her it was foggy and windy.

_____ 3. "I'm coming into the city tonight to see a play," she said.

_____ 4. Karl said, "That sounds like fun."

_____ 5. Lisa told Karl that the play had gotten very good reviews.

_____ 6. Lisa said, "I got the tickets for my birthday."

_____ 7. Karl told her to have a good time.

_____ 8. Lisa said, "Thanks. Bye."

15 Practice

Insert quotation marks and correct punctuation in the phone conversation.

Hotel clerk: Hello

Todd: Hello. I was wondering if you have a vacancy for this weekend

Hotel clerk: Yes, we do

Todd: Great. Could we get a room with a queen size bed

Hotel clerk: Sorry. The only rooms left are ones with two double beds Will that work

Todd: That's fine

Hotel clerk: Could I have your credit card number to hold the room

Todd: Here you are. It's 333 2121 4646 0000

Hotel clerk: Thank you sir. We'll see you this weekend

16 Practice

Match the quotation with the famous person who said it. Then write sentences in quoted speech using correct punctuation. Try to put *said* in different positions.

_____ 1. Most folks are as happy as they make up their minds to be.

_____ 2. I think, therefore, I am.

_____ 3. Everyone will be famous for 15 minutes.

_____ 4. Give a man a fish and you feed him for a day. Teach him how to fish and you feed him for a lifetime.

_____ 5. A journey of a thousand miles begins with a single step.

a. Andy Warhol

b. Lao Tzu

c. Confucius

d. Rene Descartes

e. Abraham Lincoln

1. _____

_____.

2. _____

_____.

3. _____

_____.

4. _____

_____.

5. _____

_____.

Noun Clauses and Reported Speech

17 Practice

What are some things your parents and friends always say? Use correct punctuation.

1. My grandfather always said, _"If you lie down with dogs, you'll get up with fleas."_

2. My dad always says, _____

3. My mom always says, _____

4. My brother/sister says, _____

5. My best friend always says, _____

11e Reported Speech: Statements

Student Book p. 328

18 Practice

Read the sentences. Write *Q* next to the sentence if the statement is quoted speech. Write *R* if it is reported speech.

_____ 1. "The new train schedule starts tomorrow," said Kim.

_____ 2. The paper said the train schedule started the next day.

_____ 3. It also said there would be fewer parking spaces at the station.

_____ 4. The reporter said, "There will be fewer parking spaces."

_____ 5. "Ticket prices are going up," said my neighbor.

_____ 6. My neighbor told me that ticket prices were going up.

_____ 7. The paper stated that routes would be cut.

_____ 8. Mr. Rankin said, "Routes will be cut."

_____ 9. I heard that the old station was being torn down.

_____ 10. My bus driver said, "The old station is being torn down."

19 Practice

James Smith, a wealthy man who is not well liked, has disappeared. The police question his girlfriend, son, butler, and ex-wife. When the police officers report the interviews, change the quoted speech into reported speech.

1. His girlfriend said, "I hate him! He ruined my life. I wish he were dead."

   His girlfriend told us that she hated James Smith and that he

   had ruined her life. She told us that she wished he were dead.

2. His son said, "Father? I don't have a father. He left my sister and me when we were young and only came around once or twice a year. I hope he stays missing."

_____

_____.

3. His ex-wife said, "I haven't seen James since our divorce became final many years ago. I don't know where he is or what he's doing, and I don't care." _____

_____

_____.

4. His butler said, "I'm not sure what his plans were yesterday. He is a very private man, and he rarely confides in me. He left the house around 9:00 in the morning yesterday, and he hasn't returned. That's why I called you." _____

_____

_____.

20 **Practice**

Read the following situations. Then rewrite the quoted speech as reported speech.

1. Yesterday, Stephanie told her officemate, Kurt, about her vacation plans.

"Last year we spent our vacation in Thailand. We thought about going back this year, but we decided to go camping instead. We're not leaving today. We're probably going to leave early tomorrow."

Later, Kurt is telling another officemate about the conversation:

Stephanie told me _that the year before they had spent their vacation_

in Thailand.

_____

_____

2. Last night's news announcer said, "Millions of gallons of water have flooded farms near Highway 4 this morning. A levee gave way, and engineers have been studying the problem to determine the cause for the collapse. Workers have been working nonstop since this morning. We're going to join our correspondent who is live at the scene."

Did you hear the news last night? The announcer said _____

_____

_____

_____

3. Tiffany, a 16-year-old high school student, is having a conversation with another girl from school on the subway home.

Melanie:	I saw you talking with Chad.
Tiffany:	I was not talking with Chad. He was talking with me.
Melanie:	Well, he's my boyfriend, and I want you to stay away from him.
Tiffany:	As if I'm interested! I was just giving him the English homework assignment. You need to get a life!

Later that night, Tiffany is talking to her friend Julie about the conversation:

Melanie said that she _____

_____

_____

_____

_____

_____

4. Doug is telling his roommate about some family problems:

"I have to drop out of school because my parents' business isn't doing very well. I need to get a job and help them. I'll finish the semester, and then I'm going to move back home. I wish I could continue studying, but I can't."

Doug's roommate is telling his girlfriend about Doug's situation:

Doug said that he _____

_____

_____

_____

_____

Practice

Read the reported statements. Rewrite them as quoted speech.

A. Bob is explaining why he had to cancel his annual cookout this year:

The Andersons told me they couldn't come because one of their children was sick. Ms. Washington, from next door, had already made plans with her daughter. Our other next-door neighbors remembered that they were going to be out of town, and Nancy told me she had a headache and wasn't feeling well.

1. The Andersons said, "We are so sorry! We can't come because one
of our children is sick."

2. Ms. Washington explained, _____

3. The neighbors said, _____

4. Nancy told Bob, _____

B. Dale is talking to John about a conversation he had with Ted, the new hire:

I told him his work hadn't been up to par and that we'd hired him because of his previous experience, but we needed him to be much more proactive. I then told him that we would revisit this issue in three months and reevaluate at that point.

1. Dale said, _____

_____

2. Dale then said, _____

_____

C. Stan is talking to his brother about his girlfriend, Angie.

I told her that things had been bad for a while and that I thought we should break up. She said she knew things were bad but she thought that they would get better. I told her I wasn't sure about that, but that we could take a break and see what happened.

1. Stan said, _____

_____

2. Angie said, _____

_____

3. Stan then said, _____

_____

22 Practice

Rewrite the answers from Practice 17 as reported speech.

1. My grandfather often told me *that if I lay down with dogs, I'd get up with fleas.*

2. My dad often told me _____
   _____.

3. My mom often told me _____
   _____.

4. My brother/sister often told me _____
   _____.

5. My best friend always told me _____
   _____.

23 Practice

Answer the questions using reported speech.

1. What has your teacher told you about using reported speech?
   _____
   _____.

2. What did your boy/girl/best friend tell you the last time you spoke?
   _____
   _____.

3. Look at your last email message. Who was it from, and what did he/she say?
   _____
   _____.

4. What did your house/roommate tell you last week?
   _____
   _____.

5. Do you have a cell phone? Who was your last call from, and what did that person say?
   _____
   _____.

6. What did the headlines in this morning's news say?

_____

_____.

7. What weather has the meteorologist predicted for today?

_____

_____.

11f Reported Speech: Questions

Student Book p. 334

24 Practice

A mother is asking her teenage daughter some questions about where she's going tonight. Read the questions, then rewrite the questions as reported speech.

1. What are you doing tonight?

2. Where is the party going to be?

3. Who is going to be there?

4. Are there going to be parents at home during the party?

5. When are you coming home?

6. Are you going to wear that?

7. Don't you have something more appropriate to wear?

Jennifer is telling her friend Mark about her mom:

1. She asked me _what I was doing tonight._ _____

2. _____

3. _____

4. _____

5. _____

6. _____

7. _____

Practice

A. You are a history teacher. Read the information on Vikings and create questions for a quiz on the reading.

The word "Viking" may come from the Swedish work *Vik* which means "bay." The Vikings were the group of people living in present day Sweden, Norway, and Denmark, who are most well known for their voyages to other countries from approximately 1060-750 B.C. The Vikings raided towns and villages across Europe, and many settled in Britain, France, and Spain. This was fairly easily done as Europe was not unified at the time. The Swedish Vikings voyaged east to Russia and the Near East, while the Danish and Norwegian Vikings went west to Europe and eventually to Iceland, Greenland, and North America.

Although many people believe they were violent, senseless, brutal people, this is just a popular misconception. Many Vikings were interested in trading and farming. Besides growing up knowing how to use a sword, Vikings were dependent on the sea for survival. The rapid attacks on unsuspecting villages were made possible by the boats the Vikings built. They were fast, long, and narrow. If there was no wind, the crew could row. They were easy to guide and could carry a large number of men.

Viking mythology states that the universe existed on a large Ash tree called "Yggdrasil," with the gods living in "Asgard" at the top of the tree, men in "Midgard," and the giants in "Jotunheim." Oden, the god of gods and men, would take the souls of men killed in battle to "Valhalla."

The age of the Vikings still captures the imagination today.

Viking Test Questions

1. _Where did the Vikings come from?_ _____

2. _____ ?

3. _____ ?

4. _____ ?

5. _____ ?

6. _____ ?

7. _____ ?

8. _____ ?

9. _____ ?

10. _____ ?

11. _____ ?

B. Now, tell the other teachers about the test questions you asked your class.

1. _I asked them where the Vikings had come from._ _____

2. _____ .

3. _____ .

4. _____ .

5. _____ .

6. _____ .

7. _____ .

8. _____ .

9. _____ .

10. _____ .

11. _____ .

Noun Clauses and Reported Speech

26 Practice

Jeff and Jeremy are brothers that were adopted by different families when they were young. Jeff posted a notice on an adoption search Website, and Jeremy responded. Now they're chatting online and finding out about each other. Read their dialogue and rewrite it as reported speech.

1. Jeff: I can't believe I found you! Where are you?

2. Jeremy: I live in Washington—the state. Where do you live?

3. Jeff: I live in Washington, too. I just moved here from Colorado.

4. Jeremy: Which city are you in?

5. Jeff: I'm in Seattle now. What city are you in?

6. Jeremy: I'm in Seattle, too. I live in Ballard.

7. Jeff: You are kidding me! I live there, too. What's your address?

8. Jeremy: I'm at 313 Main.

9. Jeff: No way! I can't believe it! Are you serious? Are you messing with me?

10. Jeremy: No! Of course not. Why?

11. Jeff: That's where I live.

12. Jeremy: Are you for real? What's your apartment number?

13. Jeff: I'm in 406B.

14. Jeremy: I'm in 503D. Are you at home?

15. Jeff: Yes.

16. Jeremy: I'm coming right down to meet you!

       Jeff: I'll be right here, man.

**Jeremy is telling a friend about his conversation with Jeff.
Be careful! Jeremy is doing the reporting, not Jeff:**

1. Jeff said he couldn't believe he'd found me and asked me where I was.

2. I told him _____.

3. _____.

4. _____.

5. _____.

6. _____.

7. _____ .

8. _____ .

9. _____ .

10. _____ .

11. _____ .

12. _____ .

13. _____ .

14. _____ .

15. _____ .

16. _____ .

11g Reported Commands, Requests, Offers, Advice, Invitations, and Warnings

Student Book p. 336

27 Practice

Sylvia has started working with a personal trainer. Her trainer has given her some advice. Rewrite the direct quotations as reported commands, advice, invitations, and warnings using appropriate verbs from the list. Answers may vary.

advise	promise	tell
ask	suggest	warn
invite		

1. You should warm up every day on the treadmill for 15 minutes.

   My trainer advised me to warm up every day on the treadmill for 15 minutes.

2. It's a good idea to do some arm work every other day. _____

   _____ .

3. Let's focus on abs every day. _____

   _____ .

4. Don't push yourself too much at the beginning. _____

   _____ .

5. Don't continue if your knees start hurting. _____

_____.

6. Follow my directions carefully so you don't get hurt. _____

_____.

7. Try drinking a glass of water before we start. _____

_____.

8. Please tell me if you don't understand something. _____

_____.

9. I'm running in a marathon next month. You could come watch if you like. _____

_____.

10. I will help you look and feel 100% better in just six weeks. _____

_____.

28 Practice

Joseph is telling his friends what his parents said to him last night. Write his parents' direct quotations. Answers may vary slightly.

"They are so bogus. First they warned me to stop hanging around with you guys because you're a 'bad influence'. Then they threatened to take away my computer if my grades don't improve. Get this. They offered to get me a tutor! I'm not stupid; I'm just bored. Then they warned me not to do drugs. As if! Only losers do drugs. They told me to be home at 10:30 during the week and at 12:00 on Fridays and Saturdays. I'm not a baby for crying out loud. Then, they offered to pay for college if I make these changes."

1. *"Stop hanging around friends who are a bad influence*

on you."

2. _____.

3. _____.

4. _____.

5. _____.

6. _____.

Practice

Do you like salsa and chips? Read this recipe for homemade salsa. Then report what the recipe says to do. Use *says* and *warns* in your sentences.

from the kitchen of _____

Salsa

Put 2 large tomatoes in boiling water for 1 minute. Take them out and remove the skins. Squeeze out the seeds and cut up the flesh into small pieces. Put 1 or 2 jalapeño peppers over a gas flame or in the broiler. Don't let them burn. Take them off the flame when they turn black. Peel the jalapeños and cut them into small pieces. Remove their seeds and ribs. Wash your hands immediately. Don't touch your eyes! Peel and cut up 1 onion. Put the tomatoes, onion, and peppers into a bowl. Cut up a large clove of garlic and add to the bowl. Add some cilantro, lime juice, salt, and pepper. Serve salsa with chips. Enjoy!

1. The recipe says _to put two large tomatoes in boiling water for one minute._

2. _____.

3. _____.

4. _____.

5. _____.

6. _____.

7. _____.

8. _____.

9. _____.

Noun Clauses and Reported Speech

10. _____ .

11. _____ .

12. _____ .

13. _____ .

14. _____ .

15. _____ .

30 | Practice

Mr. Hogan has had a heart attack. Write advice and warnings from his doctor.

1. *Stop smoking.* _____

2. _____ .

3. _____ .

4. _____ .

5. _____ .

6. _____ .

Now rewrite the warnings as reported speech.

1. *My doctor warned me to stop smoking.* _____

2. _____ .

3. _____ .

4. _____ .

5. _____ .

6. _____ .

11h The Subjunctive in Noun Clauses

Student Book p. 338

31 | Practice

Read the information for an infomercial. Underline the subjunctive in noun clauses.

You have never seen a skin cream like this before, and using this line is so easy! The makers suggest that you apply the lotion once in the morning and once before bedtime for best results. We promise you will be amazed. We ask that you try the product free for 30 days, and if you decide this skin care line is not for you, we simply request that you notify us, but keep the product as our gift to you!

32 Practice

A coach is giving the team a pre-game pep talk. Write sentences using the subjunctive and the prompts.

1. owner / insist / to be out there early

   The owner insists that you be out there early.

2. fans / demand / to give 110%

   _____.

3. I / recommend / to hit them hard

   _____.

4. your teammates / expect / not to let up

   _____.

5. the offensive coach / advise / to remember their defense is weak

   _____.

6. competitive spirit / require / to go for this win

   _____.

33 Practice

Complete the sentences with your own ideas.

1. It's crucial that a child _____.

2. It's vital that a police officer _____.

3. It's necessary that a writer _____.

4. It's important that a friend _____.

5. It's desirable that a good manager _____.

6. It's advisable that I _____.

SELF-TEST

A   Choose the best answer, A, B, C, or D, to complete the sentence. Mark your answer by darkening the oval with the same letter.

1. Have you gotten any news?

   A. I'm afraid not.   Ⓐ Ⓑ Ⓒ Ⓓ
   B. I'm not afraid.
   C. I hope so.
   D. I don't hope so.

2. The clerk asked Jeff _____.

   A. what does he want   Ⓐ Ⓑ Ⓒ Ⓓ
   B. does he want a receipt
   C. if or not he wanted a receipt
   D. if he wanted a receipt or not

3. Jorge said, "I'll see you later. I have to go now."

   A. Jorge told he would   Ⓐ Ⓑ Ⓒ Ⓓ
   see us later and that
   he had to leave then.
   B. Jorge told us I will see you later and
   that I have to leave now.
   C. Jorge told us he will see us later and
   that he will have to leave then.
   D. Jorge told us he would see us later
   and that he had to leave then.

4. I asked her _____.

   A. where did she get   Ⓐ Ⓑ Ⓒ Ⓓ
   the information
   B. if did she get the information
   C. where she had gotten the information
   D. did she get the information

5. "Please, don't do that again," said Peter.

   A. Peter asked me do   Ⓐ Ⓑ Ⓒ Ⓓ
   not do that again.
   B. Peter asked me not do that again.
   C. Peter asked me not to do that again.
   D. Peter asked not do that again.

6. The building manager requested that ___.

   A. Charles not return   Ⓐ Ⓑ Ⓒ Ⓓ
   B. Charles doesn't return
   C. Charles didn't return
   D. Charles do not return

7. "Have you finished yet?" asked Beth.

   A. Beth wanted to know   Ⓐ Ⓑ Ⓒ Ⓓ
   if I've finished yet.
   B. Beth wanted to know
   if I'd finished yet.
   C. Beth wanted to know if
   or not I'd finished yet.
   D. Beth wanted to know I'd finished yet.

8. "I'll make dinner when I get home."

   A. Junko promised she   Ⓐ Ⓑ Ⓒ Ⓓ
   will make dinner when we get home.
   B. Junko promised make dinner.
   C. Junko promised to make dinner.
   D. Junko promised I'll make dinner when
   I get home.

9. He said he didn't know who'd be there.

   A. Ed said, "He didn't   Ⓐ Ⓑ Ⓒ Ⓓ
   know who would be there."
   B. Ed said, "He doesn't know
   who would be there."
   C. Ed said, "I didn't know
   who will be there."
   D. Ed said, "I don't know
   who will be there."

10. Are you finished packing?

    A. I think so.   Ⓐ Ⓑ Ⓒ Ⓓ
    B. I'm afraid.
    C. I don't hope so.
    D. I don't think not.

B Find the underlined word or phrase, A, B, C, or D, that is incorrect. Mark your answer by darkening the oval with the same letter.

1. Jason <u>said</u> me he <u>would</u> meet us at the
   A   B
   restaurant, but that he <u>couldn't</u> <u>stay</u> long.
                            C   D

   Ⓐ Ⓑ Ⓒ Ⓓ

2. The police officer <u>asked</u> me <u>if or not</u> I
                       A   B
   <u>knew</u> how fast <u>I'd been going</u>.
    C   D

   Ⓐ Ⓑ Ⓒ Ⓓ

3. <u>That</u> you don't know how to do it
   A
   <u>doesn't bother</u> me, but you <u>told</u> me
    B   C
   you <u>do</u>.
        D

   Ⓐ Ⓑ Ⓒ Ⓓ

4. First she <u>asked</u> me <u>what</u> time it was, and
              A   B
   then she <u>asked</u> me <u>can</u> I give her a ride.
             C   D

   Ⓐ Ⓑ Ⓒ Ⓓ

5. They <u>offered</u> <u>help</u> us move, but I <u>told</u>
          A   B   C
   them we <u>had</u> enough people.
            D

   Ⓐ Ⓑ Ⓒ Ⓓ

6. I'm <u>not sure</u> what <u>do</u> they do or <u>if</u> they
        A   B   C
   <u>have</u> jobs.
    D

   Ⓐ Ⓑ Ⓒ Ⓓ

7. <u>Did</u> he <u>ask</u> <u>what's</u> <u>your name was</u>?
   A   B   C   D

   Ⓐ Ⓑ Ⓒ Ⓓ

8. <u>It's</u> <u>urgent</u> <u>whether</u> she <u>is</u> at the
   A   B   C   D
   auditorium before 8:30 tonight.

   Ⓐ Ⓑ Ⓒ Ⓓ

9. Leila <u>threatened</u> not <u>come</u>, but I <u>offered</u>
          A   B   C
   <u>to give</u> her a ride.
    D

   Ⓐ Ⓑ Ⓒ Ⓓ

10. The mayor <u>wasn't</u> sure <u>whether</u> he <u>will</u> be
               A   B   C
    re-elected <u>or not</u>.
               D

    Ⓐ Ⓑ Ⓒ Ⓓ

UNIT 12 ADJECTIVE CLAUSES

12a Adjective Clauses with Subject Relative Pronouns

Student Book p. 350

1 | Practice

Write sentences using the prompts and adjective clauses with *who, that,* or *which*.

1. Ally / suffer from allergies

   _Ally is a woman who/that suffers from allergies_____.

2. athletes / exercise regularly

   _____.

3. company / allow its employees to work at home

   _____.

4. he / listen to all kinds of music

   _____.

5. laptop / use the new operating system

   _____.

6. bad drivers / run red lights and don't use their turn signals

   _____.

7. apartment / have high ceilings

   _____.

8. you (singular) / watch a lot of movies

   _____.

9. you (plural) / watch a lot of TV

   _____.

10. book / sit on the top shelf

    _____.

Practice

Give people in the photo names. Then complete sentences about them using adjective clauses beginning with *who* or *that*.

4. _____

3. _____

2. _____

5. _____

6. _____

7. _____

1. <u>*Sherry*</u>   8. _____

1. <u>*Sherry is the woman who is sitting on the sofa.*</u>

2. _____.

3. _____.

4. _____.

5. _____.

6. _____.

7. _____.

8. _____.

12b Adjective Clauses with Object Relative Pronouns

Student Book p. 353

3 Practice

Read the sentences. Complete them with *that* if it is necessary. Leave the line blank if it is not necessary. Write if the relative pronoun is a subject or an object.

1. That's the man _*that*_ stole my wallet.   _subject_

2. It was the wallet _____ my roommate gave me.   _____

3. The police officer _____ took the report eventually
   found my wallet.   _____

4. Can I borrow the notes for the class _____ I missed today?   _____

5. She's the same teacher _____ teaches art history.   _____

6. Why aren't you wearing the blouse _____ you
   bought yesterday?   _____

7. The one _____ has the red flowers? It's too hot.   _____

8. No, the one _____ was in the window.   _____

9. The people _____ shop at that mall must be wealthy.   _____

10. I don't remember the last time _____ my roommate
    did the dishes.   _____

4 Practice

Write sentences using the prompts, object relative pronouns, and your own ideas.

1. a bracelet / a person

   A bracelet is something that/which a

   person wears on his or her wrist.

2. a masterpiece / an artist

   _____.

3. a speech / a speaker   _____.

4. a decision / you   _____.

5. a watermelon / people   _____.

6. a crown / a queen or king   _____.

7. a parachute / skydivers   _____.

8. a water tank / a town   _____.

9. a landmark / travelers   _____.

10. a bestseller / customers   _____.

5 Practice

Answer the questions with your own ideas. Write complete sentences.

1. Who is the person that you admire the most? _____

2. What are three areas that you'd like to improve in professionally? _____
_____.

3. What is a goal that you're working toward? _____
_____.

4. What's a situation that you're concerned about? _____
_____.

5. What is a situation that you don't understand? _____
_____.

12c Adjective Clauses with *Whose*
Student Book p. 356

6 Practice

Read the sentences. Rewrite them as two sentences.

1. My friend whose son attends the academy lives in Los Angeles.

   My friend lives in Los Angeles. His/her son attends the academy.

2. We've studied the philosopher whose ideas were revolutionary for his time. _____
_____
_____

3. They fired the executive whose salary was the highest. _____
_____

4. She married a man whose first language is Spanish. _____
_____

5. Karina doesn't get along with some people whose politics are different from hers.

_____

_____

6. That's the model whose face is on every magazine cover this month. _____

_____

_____

7. Justin met the neighbors whose dog keeps barking all the time. _____

_____

8. Peter is my friend whose life was saved by a kidney transplant. _____

_____

9. The jury convicted the defendant whose greed got him caught in the first place.

_____

_____

7 Practice

Ed Barnes is a candidate for political office. Read his speech and rewrite it using adjective clauses with _whose_. Possessive nouns and pronouns are underlined as clues.

(1) My opponent's attitude bothers me. (2) His lack of foresight has lead this country into near bankruptcy. (3) His continued disregard for the public's welfare is shocking and his denials of any wrongdoing trouble me, and they should trouble you.

(4) My only interest is seeing everyone in this community enjoying economic prosperity. (5) My leadership skills will move us to that end. (6) My team of experts has assured me that we have a very good chance of beating the incumbent.

(7) Your opinion matters to me. Remember to vote in this next election. (8) Your vote is very important.

1. _I am running against an opponent whose attitude bothers me._

2. _____.

3. _____ .

4. _____ .

5. _____ .

6. _____ .

7. _____ .

8. _____ .

8 Practice

When Joe left the office this afternoon, he discovered that someone had let the air out of his tires. Read about his coworkers. Write two sentences for each, saying if he or she may have or may not have done it. Use *whose* or subject or object relative pronouns in the adjective clauses.

1. Woman #1 - can't stand Joe because she was his temporary supervisor and trained Joe for the job. When he became her supervisor, he fired her. Her last day was today.

   The woman who was fired may have done it because she's angry.   (OR)

   The woman who trained Joe may have done it because she's angry.

2. Man #1 - doesn't like Joe because today he yelled at him in front of the other team members, which was unnecessary, especially considering he had recently loaned Joe $100. He's been in his office since early this morning.

   _____ .

   _____ .

3. Woman #2 - doesn't respect Joe because he took credit for a project she completed. Today, she missed an important conference call because he told her it was scheduled one hour later.

   _____ .

   _____ .

4. Man #2 - is angry with Joe because when he came back from vacation yesterday, Joe had taken one of his main accounts. Additionally, Joe asked him to work late this afternoon, but Joe left the office early.

   _____ .

   _____ .

Practice

What qualities and characteristics do you look for in a friend? Write sentences with adjective clauses using *whose* and words from the list or your own ideas.

age	ideas	physical appearance
background	income	sense of humor
educational level	job	values

1. *I like people whose values are similar to my own.*

2. _____.

3. _____.

4. _____.

5. _____.

6. _____.

7. _____.

8. _____.

9. _____.

12d *When, Where, Why,* and *That* as Relative Pronouns
Student Book p. 358

10 **Practice**

Lucy and Dirk are showing photos and telling their neighbors about a trip. Read their sentences and combine them in two ways: once using *where* and once using *that + in, at, on,* or *to.*

1. We visited the battlefield. Thousands of soldiers died there.

   a. *We visited the battlefield where thousands of soldiers died.*

   b. *We visited the battlefield that thousands of soldiers died on.*

2. We saw the house. The religious leader was born there.

   _____.

   _____.

3. This is the clock tower. We had our picture taken there.

_____ .

_____ .

4. We chose a small town. Fewer tourists were there.

_____ .

_____ .

5. We stayed at a hotel. The royal family had stayed there the week before.

_____ .

_____ .

6. This is the restaurant. Our friends took us there.

_____ .

_____ .

7. This is the square. We lost our traveler's checks there.

_____ .

_____ .

8. Next year we'd like to go to a place. The weather is a little warmer.

_____ .

_____ .

II Practice

Complete the sentences with _when_ and your own ideas.

1. That was the birthday _when my uncle fell into the pool._ _____

2. Do you remember the year _____ ?

3. The night _____ was terrible.

4. I'll never forget the time _____ .

5. The New Year's Eve _____ was a lot of fun.

6. My most memorable experience was the summer _____ .

12 Practice

Combine the sentences in two ways using *when, where, that,* or *why.* You may use prepositions with *that.*

1. That was the party. I met my wife.

   That was the party where I met my wife.

   That was the party that I met my wife at.

2. It was the fall. I started teaching at the university.

   _____.

   _____.

3. We got married in the same place. We met there.

   _____.

   _____.

4. That is the reason. We went to the same place on our second honeymoon.

   _____.

   _____.

5. We moved to the city. Her family is there.

   _____.

   _____.

6. It is the reason. We moved to the city.

   _____.

   _____.

13 Practice

Answer the questions. Use *why* in your adjective clause.

1. What's the reason (why) people go to war? _____.

2. What's the reason (why) people should be concerned about the environment?

   _____.

3. Do you know the reason (why) the moon looks larger at the horizon than when it

   rises? _____.

4. What's the reason (why) you're studying English? _____.

12e Defining and Nondefining Adjective Clauses

Student Book p. 361

14 Practice

Read the sentences. Write *D* next to the sentence if the adjective clause is defining. Write *ND* if the adjective clause is nondefining.

_____ 1. Lilacs, which are my mother's favorite flower, don't grow well in this climate.

_____ 2. The lilacs which mom planted last year are just starting to bloom.

_____ 3. Whole wheat bread, which is bread that has a lot of natural fiber, is good for you.

_____ 4. The whole wheat bread that's made in that bakery is kind of expensive, but delicious.

_____ 5. Children who don't eat breakfast don't do as well in school as those who do.

_____ 6. Children, who need good nutrition to do well in school, have a lot more homework these days than in the past.

_____ 7. The paper which is used to print photos is more expensive than regular printer paper.

_____ 8. Paper, which is made from wood pulp and various chemicals, is processed in paper mills.

_____ 9. Antique jewelry, which is jewelry 100 years old or older, can be expensive to buy.

_____ 10. The antique necklace that my grandmother gave me needs to be repaired.

15 Practice

Read the statements. Underline the subject.

1. <u>Toys,</u> which can help children learn, have changed dramatically in the last 100 years.

2. <u>Toys that have very small parts</u> should not be given to very young children.

3. Guacamole, which is made from avocados, lime, cilantro, garlic, salt, and pepper, is very popular in Mexican restaurants.

4. The guacamole which my husband makes is out of this world!

5. The grammar exercises which are in this book are fun and easy!

6. Grammar exercises, which are designed to help people learn language, involve rules.

7. Garlic, which some people believe has medical properties, is easy to grow.

8. The garlic which you can buy crushed in a jar has a different taste from fresh garlic.

Practice

Underline and put commas around the nondefining adjective clauses.

Some of the earliest ways to measure time were the use of obelisks in Egypt. Obelisks, which are tall four-sided towers, cast shadows which people could use to measure different times of day. Later, people used water clocks which measured time by how long it took for water to leak from one container to another. Water clocks, which didn't depend on the sun, moon, or stars, had markings in them to indicate time periods as the containers filled with the water. Candles, which were also used to mark the passage of time, burned to marks made along the side. In the 1400s, mechanical clocks, which use a mainspring and balance wheel, were introduced. In 1657, Christiaan Huygens built the first clock that used a pendulum. In 1884, many countries adopted Greenwich, England, as the Prime Meridian, which indicates zero degrees longitude. In the 1920s, quartz clocks were developed. Quartz crystals, which can produce regular electric pulses, were found to be more accurate in keeping time than clocks which contained gears.

12f Using *Which* to Refer to an Entire Clause

Student Book p. 364

17 Practice

Combine the sentences with *which*.

1. Martha is in really good shape. This makes her happy.

   <u>Martha is in really good shape, which makes her happy</u>.

2. Martha's running partner, Julia, has entered them in a triathlon for this fall. This has surprised Martha. _____

   _____.

3. Martha and Julia are going to have only five months to train before the triathlon. This makes Martha a little nervous. _____

   _____.

4. She and Julia have run races together, but they haven't done the swimming or cycling before. This worries her. _____

   _____.

5. Julia has done several triathlons. This is why she knows that they can do it.

   _____.

6. Martha is an excellent swimmer. This will be when she makes good time in the race. _____

   _____.

7. Julia has organized training rides to get Martha ready for the cycling part of the race. This will build Martha's cycling stamina. _____

   _____.

8. After the triathlon, they are going to take a vacation for two weeks. This is just long enough to recover! _____

   _____.

18 Practice

Complete the sentences with *which* and your own ideas.

1. He had to drive for 12 hours, <u>which was exhausting.</u>

2. We didn't have enough sugar for the cake, _____.

3. Our goldfish died, _____.

4. No one talked to us at the reception, _____.

5. The mechanic said the repair would cost $900.00, _____.

6. The doctor said there was nothing seriously wrong, _____.

7. My daughter wants to play the drums, _____.

8. Jeff made my favorite dessert, _____.

9. No one was hurt in the accident, _____.

10. My company is eliminating our medical insurance, _____.

19 Practice

Complete the sentences with your own ideas.

1. I _____, which _____.

2. My friends _____, which _____.

3. My parents _____, which _____.

4. My grandfather _____, which _____.

5. My teacher _____, which _____.

12g Reduced Adjective Clauses

Student Book p. 367

20 Practice

Underline the reduced adjective clauses (the adjective phrases).

Before the existence of money, barter, the exchange of goods and services for other goods and services, was the primary means of acquisition. In China, from approximately 9000 to 6000 B.C., cattle and grain were used for barter. From about 1200 B.C., many cultures used cowry shells, the shell from an animal found in the Pacific and Indian Oceans. This practice lasted for many hundreds of years. In 1000 B.C., China started producing coins made of metal, typically having a hole in them so as to be put on a string. In the country of Lydia, now part of Turkey, the first modern coins, made from silver and having a round shape, were manufactured. In China in 118 B.C., leather money appeared. This leather strip was the predecessor for paper notes, also appearing for the first time in China. In North America in the 1500s, "wampum," strings of shell beads, was used by the Native Americans for trade, as gifts, and other purposes. In later years, England and the United States adopted the gold standard, abandoned in the United States after the Great Depression. Today people rely on bank cards representing how much money a person has for many of their daily transactions.

21 Practice

Reduce the adjective clauses. Rewrite the sentences.

1. On November 7, 1940, the Tacoma Narrows Bridge, which was the third longest bridge in the world, collapsed after only four months.

   On November 7, 1940, the Tacoma Narrows Bridge, the third longest bridge in the world, collapsed after only four months.

2. The bridge, which was located on the Tacoma Narrows, was light and flexible.

   _____

   _____.

3. The bridge, which was called "Galloping Gertie," would move when the wind blew at relatively low speeds.

_____

_____.

4. No one thought the bridge, which had been designed by a well-known engineer, was dangerous.

_____

_____.

5. On November 7, 1940, the wind, which had a speed of about 42 miles per hour, caused the bridge to oscillate violently.

_____

_____.

6. The people who were driving in the two cars that were on the bridge at the time of its collapse got away safely.

_____

_____.

7. The collapse, which was seen and documented by many people, taught engineers about the unique properties of suspension bridges.

_____

_____.

22 Practice

Expand the reduced adjective clauses.

1. People thinking about going on a low-carb diet should talk to their doctors first.

   People who are thinking about going on a low-carb diet

   should talk to their doctors first.

2. The light coming into the west window keeps the living room warm in the afternoon.

   _____

   _____.

3. People unhappy in their current careers should seek advice from a counselor.

   _____

   _____.

4. Do you see the men talking on the corner? The one on the right is my boss.

   _____.

   _____.

5. Buildings built before the 1900s are protected under landmark status in this town.

   _____.

   _____.

6. I can't eat products made with peanuts.

   _____.

7. My dad doesn't listen to any music recorded after 1990.

   _____.

8. Merchants selling jewelry on the street must have a permit.

   _____.

9. Does anyone know what happened to the money left on the table?

   _____.

10. The people living in the downstairs apartment just moved out.

   _____.

23 Practice

Complete the sentences with your own ideas.

1. Shoes made in Italy _are of a very good quality._____

2. Music coming out of Europe these days _____.

3. Movies from Hollywood _____.

4. Soccer players making a lot of money_____.

5. A car alarm going off in the middle of the night _____.

6. Cars consuming a lot of gasoline _____.

7. People downloading music from the Internet _____.

8. Teenagers using drugs _____.

9. Tourists looking for an interesting place to visit _____.

10. Tea grown in Japan _____.

SELF-TEST

A   **Choose the best answer, A, B, C, or D, to complete the sentence. Mark your answer by darkening the oval with the same letter.**

1. I have a friend _____ son is on TV.

   A. who   Ⓐ Ⓑ Ⓒ Ⓓ
   B. whose
   C. that
   D. when

2. We just passed the hospital _____ I was born.

   A. where   Ⓐ Ⓑ Ⓒ Ⓓ
   B. which
   C. that
   D. when

3. Sunset is the time _____ the birds are their most active.

   A. where   Ⓐ Ⓑ Ⓒ Ⓓ
   B. which
   C. that
   D. when

4. Calendars are tools _____ track the passage of time.

   A. where   Ⓐ Ⓑ Ⓒ Ⓓ
   B. who
   C. that
   D. when

5. The typewriter, _____ was the predecessor to the modern word processor, was invented in 1873.

   A. where   Ⓐ Ⓑ Ⓒ Ⓓ
   B. who
   C. that
   D. which

6. Donald doesn't have a computer, _____ puts him at a disadvantage with his coworkers.

   A. where   Ⓐ Ⓑ Ⓒ Ⓓ
   B. who
   C. that
   D. which

7. The house _____ was broken into last Saturday night.

   A. at the end of the   Ⓐ Ⓑ Ⓒ Ⓓ
       block
   B. where at the end of the block
   C. that at the end of the block
   D. which at the end of the block

8. I love the smell of bread _____ in the oven.

   A. bakes   Ⓐ Ⓑ Ⓒ Ⓓ
   B. which bake
   C. that bake
   D. baking

9. Stan prefers watching films _____ Japan.

   A. where   Ⓐ Ⓑ Ⓒ Ⓓ
   B. whose
   C. that are from
   D. which

10. The bus _____ now is an express one. You can get downtown in 20 minutes.

   A. come   Ⓐ Ⓑ Ⓒ Ⓓ
   B. coming
   C. that come
   D. which come

B **Find the underlined word or phrase, A, B, C, or D, that is incorrect. Mark your answer by darkening the oval with the same letter.**

1. Lava lamps, that were loved in the 1960s,
   A
   are popular again. People nostalgic for the
   B   **C**
   past may invest in one of these retro items.
   D

   Ⓐ Ⓑ Ⓒ Ⓓ

2. The Suez Canal, which links two seas, may
   A
   have been planned in ancient Egypt.
   B
   The idea was revisited by Napoleon, who
   C
   engineers made calculations, later found
   D
   to be faulty.

   Ⓐ Ⓑ Ⓒ Ⓓ

3. Apples sold in the supermarket don't taste
   A
   as good as those who sold at an orchard.
   B   **C**   **D**

   Ⓐ Ⓑ Ⓒ Ⓓ

4. The campground when we spent our last
   A
   vacation was destroyed by a tornado that
   B   **C**
   touched down last week.
   D

   Ⓐ Ⓑ Ⓒ Ⓓ

5. My dad, who's not feeling well, just called
   A   **B**
   me. His leg, injuring when he fell down
   C
   last year, was bothering him.
   D

   Ⓐ Ⓑ Ⓒ Ⓓ

6. Shrimp, also known as prawns, are high in
   A
   cholesterol. Patients telling to lower their
   B
   cholesterol levels by their doctors, may
   have to avoid eating shrimp.
   C   **D**

   Ⓐ Ⓑ Ⓒ Ⓓ

7. Mt. Rushmore, which is locating in South
   A   **B**
   Dakota, is visited by tourists every year.
   C   **D**

   Ⓐ Ⓑ Ⓒ Ⓓ

8. The terms agreed to last year have been
   A
   changed to reflect the cost of living. This
   B
   increase, which was 1.5%, has negatively
   C
   impacted manufacturing, that is bad news.
   D

   Ⓐ Ⓑ Ⓒ Ⓓ

9. Our professor, whose usually very busy,
   A
   stayed after class to answer questions
   B
   that we had about our test tomorrow.
   C   **D**

   Ⓐ Ⓑ Ⓒ Ⓓ

10. Peach Melba, a dessert named for an
    A
    opera singer, was created by Escoffier.
    B
    The dessert, made from peaches, was one
    C
    of two food items naming for the singer.
    D

    Ⓐ Ⓑ Ⓒ Ⓓ

UNIT 13 ADVERB CLAUSES

13a Adverb Clauses of Time

Student Book p. 380

1 Practice

Read the short passages about successful individuals. Then match the sentence halves to create complete sentences about their lives.

A.

Phil Barsky is a filmmaker who has recently had some success. His new film *Alone* was just nominated for an Academy Award. The awards will be presented next week, and critics predict that Barsky will be taking home an Oscar. Barsky hasn't always been so successful, however. The film *Alone* was what made people finally pay attention to him. In the past, he has made small movies that failed at the box office or that were never released. His new film suggests he has come a long way from his days as a production

assistant. He has come an even longer way from his previous job: he used to be a

dishwasher at Planet Hollywood in Los Angeles!

_____ 1. When the Academy Awards are presented next week,	**a.** before he made movies.
_____ 2. Until he made the movie *Alone*,	**b.** he was a production assistant.
_____ 3. Barsky was a dishwasher at Planet Hollywood	**c.** they failed at the box office.
_____ 4. Before he was a filmmaker,	**d.** Barsky may win an Oscar.
_____ 5. Whenever he released his previous movies,	**e.** nobody paid attention to Barsky's work.

B.

In her childhood, Dr. Leslie Thorne was always fascinated by outer space. She used to look at the moon and the stars through a telescope that her father had given her for her tenth birthday. In high school, she took the most advanced math and science classes, and her teachers encouraged her to study astronomy and physics in college. Dr. Thorne worked hard, studied for many years, and earned a Ph.D. in astronomy. Her Ph.D. research was published last year. Immediately after that, she was asked to join an expedition in space as a researcher. She will accompany a crew of scientists on a research mission at the next shuttle launch, scheduled for June 15, 2005.

_____ **1.** When Dr. Thorne was a girl,

_____ **2.** Her father gave her a telescope

_____ **3.** Dr. Thorne took the most advanced math and science classes

_____ **4.** Dr. Thorne studied astronomy and physics

_____ **5.** After Dr. Thorne finished her Ph.D.,

_____ **6.** As soon as her Ph.D. research was published,

_____ **7.** The next time that a space shuttle is launched,

a. when she turned ten.

b. Dr. Thorne was offered an opportunity to join a research team in space.

c. when she went to college.

d. while she was in high school.

e. she was very interested in outer space.

f. Dr. Thorne will be there with a research team.

g. her research was published.

2 Practice

Read the sentences. Write *C* next to the sentence if it uses the adverb clause of time correctly. Write *I* if it uses the adverb clause of time incorrectly. Then correct the sentences with errors. There may be more than one way to correct an error.

_____ **1.** As soon as you get home please give me a call.

_____.

_____ **2.** Their car will be repaired by the time they return.

_____.

_____ **3.** As long as we have enough water, we will feel fine on our hike.

_____.

_____ **4.** Were you worried the first time when you traveled alone?

_____?

_____ **5.** Whenever I saw that movie the first time, I was very scared.

_____.

_____ **6.** The workers may go home only until the job is finished.

_____.

_____ **7.** Amy has gone to the theater every weekend, since she moved to New York.

_____.

_____ **8.** Once they get married, they will look for a house.

_____.

_____ **9.** While Susan was talking on the phone, when her dog ran out the door.

_____.

_____ **10.** Everyone watched in horror, as the dancer fell off the stage.

_____.

3 Practice

Who do you think is successful? Write a paragraph about someone's accomplishments. The person can be someone you know personally or someone who is famous. Use at least six adverb clauses of time.

_____

_____

_____

_____

_____

_____

_____

_____

13b Adverb Clauses of Reason and Result

Student Book p. 383

4 Practice

Complete the sentences by circling the correct words in parentheses. Pay attention to punctuation.

1. Yesterday I took the subway to work (so / because) my car was being repaired at the garage.

2. I planned an extra thirty minutes to get to work (so / because) the subway can be slow in the morning.

3. A lot of people take the subway to work, (so / because) the busiest time to travel is between 7:00 and 8:00 A.M.

4. The subway was almost full, (so / because) many people didn't have seats.

5. The subway stopped in the tunnel (so / because) there was a mechanical problem.

6. The tunnel was dark and the subway lights didn't work; (because / consequently) some people started to get worried.

7. Twenty minutes went by; (as a result / because of), some people started to look at their watches.

8. We were in a tunnel, (so / therefore) I couldn't call my boss on my cell phone to tell him I would be late.

9. Like the other people on the train, I was upset (because / because of) the long delay.

10. Eventually a repair car came; (therefore / so) the train was fixed and we arrived at the next station.

5 | Practice

Rewrite each pair of sentences in two ways, once using *so ... that* and once using *such (a/an) ... that*.

1. Erin and Paul dined at a new restaurant. Almost nobody else was there.

    a. *The restaurant was so new that almost nobody else was there.*

    b. *It was such a new restaurant that almost nobody else was there.*

2. The service was slow. They waited thirty minutes for their food.

    a. _____

    _____

    b. _____

    _____

3. The view was beautiful. Erin and Paul didn't mind the slow service.

    a. _____

    b. _____

4. The afternoon was warm. They did not need to wear jackets.

    a. _____

    b. _____

5. The pasta was delicious. They ate every bite of it.

    a. _____

    b. _____

6. The dessert was sweet. Erin couldn't eat all of it.

    a. _____

    b. _____

7. The bill was expensive. Paul thought there must be a mistake.

    a. _____

    b. _____

8. The restaurant was romantic. Erin and Paul decided to eat there again someday.

    a. _____

    b. _____

6 | Practice

Add the correct punctuation to each sentence. For some sentences, there may be more than one way to add punctuation. Some sentences may not need punctuation.

1. The firefighter was very brave and so he won an award.

2. Since I must go to work so early I decided to go to bed early.

3. Gil didn't understand his math homework therefore he found a math tutor.

4. Rick was upset because his brother lost his favorite tie.

5. My sister is allergic to bees as a result she has to carry medicine with her.

6. Because of the earthquake many homes were damaged.

7. It was such a long class that the students had difficulty paying attention.

8. Our flight was delayed and as a result we did not leave until the next day.

9. Beth bought the wrong size dress so she'll have to return to the store.

10. The company had to close consequently many people lost their jobs.

13c Adverb Clauses of Purpose

Student Book p. 387

7 Practice

Circle the letter of the sentence that uses an adverb clause of purpose.

1. **a.** The book was so good that I read it twice.

   b. I read the book twice so that I would remember it better.

2. **a.** I'm going to study hard so that I'll be prepared for the test.

   b. I studied so hard that I was very well prepared for the test.

3. **a.** I set the alarm clock so early that I woke up long before the test.

   b. I set the alarm clock so that I would wake up very early on the day of the test.

4. **a.** At lunch, I was so hungry that I ate two sandwiches.

   b. At lunch, I ate two sandwiches so that I wouldn't be hungry anymore.

5. **a.** Jess bought a lot of groceries so that she wouldn't have to go shopping for a long time.

   b. Jess bought so many groceries that she didn't have to go shopping for a long time.

6. **a.** Mike worked so quickly that he was able to go home early.

   b. Mike worked quickly so that he could go home early.

8 Practice

Complete the sentences with *in order to* or *so that* to show purpose, or *therefore* to show result. Add commas, semicolons, and periods where necessary.

Mariel bought a new handbag, but when she got home, she saw that the strap was

broken. _____Therefore_____, she decided to take it back to the store. She put the sales

1

receipt in her pocket _____ she could show when she bought the bag and

2

how much she paid for it. At the store, she showed the salesclerk the broken strap. She

said she had brought the bag back _____ replace it with a different one.

3

The salesclerk said she needed the receipt _____ approve the exchange.

4

Mariel looked in her pocket, but she couldn't find the receipt. Then she noticed there was

a hole in her pocket _____ the receipt must have fallen out somewhere.

5

Mariel walked back to the entrance of the store, looking at the ground _____

6

she might see the lost receipt. At last she found it just outside the door. She ran back to the salesclerk in order to give her the receipt before she lost it again. _____,
7
the salesclerk was able to exchange the handbag, and Mariel found one without a broken strap. Now whenever she buys something, she puts the sales receipt in her new handbag _____ she doesn't lose it.
8

9 | Practice

Have you ever lost something or worried about losing something? Write a paragraph of at least six sentences about your experience. Use *in order to* or *so that* to show purpose and *therefore, as a result,* or *consequently* to show result. Use the correct punctuation.

Example: *Last summer, I was the best man in my brother's wedding. My brother gave me the wedding rings so that I would be able to present them during the ceremony. I put them in my jacket pocket in order to keep them safe. . .*

_____

_____

_____

_____

_____

_____

_____

_____

_____

_____

_____

13d Adverb Clauses of Contrast

Student Book p. 389

10 Practice

Circle the correct adverb in parentheses to complete the sentences.

Every January, (when / because of) the
                              1
ground is covered with snow and the trees are

glistening with ice, our city has a Winter

Festival. For three days, people come to the

city center (so that / in order to) play winter
                          2
games, ice skate on the pond, and view the amazing ice sculptures. The ice sculptures

are the most famous part of the Winter Festival (though / because) they are made
                                                              3
by famous sculptors from different countries. Some of the sculptures are impressive

(even though / because of) their large size, (whereas / although) others are smaller
          4   **5**
but show amazing detail. For example, one sculpture of a house was very simple;

(however / whereas), it was large enough to walk in. Another sculpture I remember was
      6
of a Japanese fan that was small (so that / though) detailed.
                                          7

(So that / Therefore) the artists can make their sculptures, the weather conditions
          8
need to be just right. (Once / Although) the temperature rises above freezing, it becomes
                          9
very difficult to make ice sculptures. In addition, the sculptures don't last long

(nevertheless / when) the air gets warmer or it rains. Unfortunately, last year this is
        10
exactly what happened. The day (before / until) the festival started, it was 40 degrees
                                  11
Fahrenheit. (Even though / Because of) the warm temperature, the sculptures started to
                      12
melt. Some were melting (consequently / while) the artists were still trying to finish
                                      13
them. Snow machines were brought to the park, as well as fans blowing cold air

(so that / however) the ice wouldn't melt so quickly. Tents were constructed
      14
(in order to / because of) keep the rain off the sculptures. These efforts weren't
        15
enough, (even though / though). The ice continued to melt. (So that / Therefore),
                  16   **17**
everyone worried that there would be no ice sculptures at the festival.

On the second day of the festival, it got even warmer. (Whereas / Although) it rained
18
steadily for the next day and a half, people came to the Winter Festival anyway. The ice
artists displayed photographs of their sculptures (nevertheless / so that) people could see
19
something interesting. (However / While) everyone missed seeing the real ice sculptures,
20
most people agreed that it was nice to see the photographs. It was disappointing not to
have winter weather; (whereas / nevertheless), most people had fun anyway.
21

II Practice

**Combine each pair of sentences into one longer
sentence using the adverbs in parentheses. Use
the correct punctuation.**

1. My city, Montreal, is very cold in the winter.
   There are many fun things to do outside.
   (although, however)

   a. <u>Although my city is very cold
   in the winter, there are many
   fun things to do outside.</u>

   b. _____

   _____

2. You can go ice-skating in the park. Sometimes it is too cold for that.
   (although, nevertheless)

   a. _____

   _____

   b. _____

   _____

3. Many people like to go shopping in the underground malls. Others prefer visiting
   museums. (while, though)

   a. _____

   _____

   b. _____

   _____

4. The streets can be slippery with ice. Some people think it's romantic to ride in a horse and carriage. (even though, however)

   a. _____

   _____

   b. _____

   _____

5. It's a long drive. It's fun to go to Quebec City for the winter festival. (although, nevertheless)

   a. _____

   _____

   b. _____

   _____

6. My husband always wants to go somewhere warmer in the winter. I prefer to stay in Canada. (whereas, though)

   a. _____

   _____

   b. _____

   _____

Practice

Study the pairs of photographs. Write at least four sentences about the differences between them using adverb clauses of contrast *although, even though, though, whereas, while, nevertheless,* and *however*. Use the correct punctuation.

A.

_____

_____

_____

_____

_____

B.

_____

_____

_____

_____

_____

245

13e Adverb Clauses of Condition

Student Book p. 391

13 Practice

Rewrite the sentences using the words in parentheses. Use the correct punctuation.

Vinnie's Wraps:

Employee's Handbook

1. If it is not a special promotion day, all employees must wear black pants and a green shirt to work. (unless)

   Unless it is a special promotion day, all employees

   must wear black pants and a green shirt to work.

2. Whether or not you washed your hands before coming to work, you must wash them again before handling food. (even if)

   _____

   _____

3. Hair must be tied back and worn under a cap if it isn't above your shoulders. (unless)

   _____

   _____

4. Personal phone calls are not permitted unless it is an emergency. (only if)

   _____

   _____

5. You should talk to your supervisor if you have problems with your schedule. (in case)

   _____

   _____

6. All requests for vacation time must be in writing; it does not matter if you have talked to your supervisor first. (whether or not)

   _____

   _____

7. You may have one free meal on your shift. This is true if you work only a five-hour shift. (even if)

_____

_____

8. Food can only be consumed in the employee kitchen; however, if the restaurant is closed, you may eat in the dining room. (unless)

_____

_____

|14| Practice

Rewrite the sentences two ways with _only if_. The first time, use the _only if_ clause in the second part of the sentence. The second time, use the _only if_ clause at the beginning of the sentence. Use the correct punctuation.

1. I can buy a used car. In order to do so, I have to save $2,000.

  a. _I can buy a used car only if I save $2,000._

  b. _Only if I save $2,000 can I buy a used car._

2. I can save $2,000. In order to do so, I must stop buying things I don't need.

  a. _____

  b. _____

3. I will stop buying lunch every day. The only way I can do that is to make my lunch at home.

  a. _____

  b. _____

4. I will quit drinking expensive coffee. But I can't do that unless I stop walking past that new cafe on my way to work.

  a. _____

  b. _____

5. I will cancel my cable TV service. The only way to do that is to start reading more.

  a. _____

  b. _____

6. I can get books from the library instead of the bookstore. But I can't do this until I pay my library fine.

a. _____

b. _____

7. I'll stop using my cell phone so often. To do so, my friends will need to start calling me at home.

a. _____

b. _____

8. I could just get a second job—but I would need to have a car in order to get from one job to the other.

a. _____

b. _____

15 Practice

What rules did you have to follow when you were growing up, or what rules must you live by now? Did your parents or an older sibling make rules for you? Write six rules using adverb clauses of condition. Use the correct punctuation.

Example: *When I was growing up, my older brother was very bossy. I couldn't watch a TV show unless it was a show that he liked. I could play with him and his friends only if he was in a good mood. Even if I was very nice to him, he teased me. Only if I cried did he stop and apologize.*

_____

_____

_____

_____

_____

_____

_____

_____

13f Reduced Adverb Clauses

Student Book p. 394

16 Practice

Read the sentences. Write *AC* next to the sentence if an adverb clause is used. Write *AP* if an adverb phrase is used.

_____ **1.** After living in their apartment for two years, Carl and Adene decided to make some changes.

_____ **2.** Wanting to make some inexpensive changes, they decided to paint the walls.

_____ **3.** Before they started the project, they looked at magazines to see what colors they liked.

_____ **4.** When they looked at paint, the amount of choices they had suddenly became overwhelming.

_____ **5.** After they argued over different colors, they finally agreed to paint two walls of the living room blue and two walls yellow.

_____ **6.** They prepared the walls with white primer before applying colored paint.

_____ **7.** While painting, Adene secretly worried that the colors would look bad.

_____ **8.** Once the walls were painted, however, Adene realized that blue and yellow looked good together.

_____ **9.** Since they redecorated the living room, they have gone on to change the kitchen.

_____ **10.** Because they know how to paint a room, the job will probably go faster now.

Rewrite the sentences in Practice 16. Change adverb phrases to adverb clauses. Reduce adverb clauses to adverb phrases. If a clause cannot be reduced, write *can't reduce.*

1. *After they had lived in their apartment for two years, Carl and Adene decided to make some changes.*

2. _____

_____

3. _____

_____

4. _____

_____

5. _____

_____

6. _____

_____

7. _____

_____

8. _____

_____

9. _____

_____

10. _____

_____

18 Practice

Read the sentences. Write *C* next to the sentence if the adverb clause or phrase is used correctly. Write *I* if it is used incorrectly.

_____ **1.** Because wanting to do some research, Tom went to the library.

_____ **2.** When finished, this painting will sell for over $10,000.

_____ **3.** Since she beginning violin lessons, Yushen has learned six songs.

_____ **4.** Can you stop at the hardware store before returned home?

_____ **5.** The Robertsons talked to their son upon they learned he had failed physics.

_____ **6.** Make sure you have all the ingredients before cooking this meal.

_____ **7.** After listened to loud music at the concert, I decided that I should wear earplugs.

_____ **8.** I can't study while watching TV.

19 Practice

Write a paragraph of instructions about how to make or do something. Use one of the ideas from the list or an idea of your own. Use at least six reduced adverb clauses.

How to boil an egg   How to place an international phone call

How to download music   How to use email

How to make coffee

_____

_____

_____

_____

_____

_____

_____

_____

_____

_____

A **Choose the best answer, A, B, C, or D, to complete the sentence. Mark your answer by darkening the oval with the same letter.**

1. _____ Ed has traveled all over Latin America, he has never been to Brazil.

   A. Because   Ⓐ Ⓑ Ⓒ Ⓓ
   B. However
   C. Although
   D. So that

2. The car was _____ expensive that we couldn't consider buying it.

   A. such   Ⓐ Ⓑ Ⓒ Ⓓ
   B. such an
   C. too
   D. so

3. _____ Mr. Benson returns, I will give him your message.

   A. Until   Ⓐ Ⓑ Ⓒ Ⓓ
   B. While
   C. Once
   D. Before

4. You should look on the Internet _____ find the best deal on a car.

   A. in order that   Ⓐ Ⓑ Ⓒ Ⓓ
   B. in order to
   C. so that
   D. so to

5. You should take money for a taxi _____ you think you won't need it.

   A. in case   Ⓐ Ⓑ Ⓒ Ⓓ
   B. even if
   C. whether or not
   D. only if

6. Muriel gets angry _____ she is interrupted at work.

   A. whenever   Ⓐ Ⓑ Ⓒ Ⓓ
   B. since
   C. the next time
   D. so long as

7. Because of _____, school was cancelled for the day.

   A. the snow   Ⓐ Ⓑ Ⓒ Ⓓ
   B. it was snowing
   C. it snowed
   D. snowing

8. Jim called the phone company _____ he could have his phone repaired.

   A. such that   Ⓐ Ⓑ Ⓒ Ⓓ
   B. in order to
   C. so that
   D. because of

9. The skier broke her leg; _____, she didn't compete.

   A. however   Ⓐ Ⓑ Ⓒ Ⓓ
   B. as a result
   C. until
   D. because of

10. It's dangerous to talk on the phone _____ driving a car.

   A. you are   Ⓐ Ⓑ Ⓒ Ⓓ
   B. while you
   C. while
   D. while are

B **Find the underlined word or phrase, A, B, C, or D, that is incorrect. Mark your answer by darkening the oval with the same letter.**

1. <u>Upon learn</u> the good news, <u>I called</u> all my
   A   **B**

   friends <u>in order</u> <u>to tell them.</u>
          C   **D**

   Ⓐ Ⓑ Ⓒ Ⓓ

2. We forgot <u>to lock</u> the door <u>behind us</u>
            A   **B**

   <u>the last time</u> <u>left</u> the building.
   C   **D**

   Ⓐ Ⓑ Ⓒ Ⓓ

3. <u>As soon as</u> <u>you have</u> the time, you need
   A   **B**

   <u>to sign</u> the form <u>in order we</u> refund your
   C   **D**

   money.

   Ⓐ Ⓑ Ⓒ Ⓓ

4. <u>Because it was</u> <u>so bad TV show</u>, it
   A   **B**

   <u>was cancelled</u> <u>after only three shows</u>.
   C   **D**

   Ⓐ Ⓑ Ⓒ Ⓓ

5. The employees <u>won't be satisfied</u> <u>however</u>
                 A   **B**

   they are <u>paid fairly</u> <u>for their work.</u>
            C   **D**

   Ⓐ Ⓑ Ⓒ Ⓓ

6. Some people love hot weather, <u>whereas</u>
                                  A

   some people <u>can't stand to be</u> in the
               B

   summer heat <u>in case</u> <u>they have</u> an air
               C   **D**

   conditioner.

   Ⓐ Ⓑ Ⓒ Ⓓ

7. <u>As a result</u> it hadn't rained <u>for many weeks</u>,
   A   **B**   **C**

   wildfires <u>were destroying</u> the forests.
             D

   Ⓐ Ⓑ Ⓒ Ⓓ

8. <u>Whether or not</u> it rains, we <u>should take</u>
   A   **B**   **C**

   the umbrellas on our picnic

   <u>so we will be that prepared</u> for anything.
   D

   Ⓐ Ⓑ Ⓒ Ⓓ

9. My sister, <u>who loves music</u>, cannot sing
              A

   <u>very well</u>; <u>consequently</u>, she was asked
   B   **C**

   <u>to be</u> the lead singer in a band.
   D

   Ⓐ Ⓑ Ⓒ Ⓓ

10. <u>I'll help you</u> with your English homework
    A

    <u>only if</u> <u>help me</u> <u>to study for</u> the math test.
    B   **C**   **D**

    Ⓐ Ⓑ Ⓒ Ⓓ

UNIT 14 CONDITIONAL SENTENCES

14a Real Conditional Sentences in the Present and Future

Student Book p. 406

1 | Practice

Match the sentences with the functions of the present real conditional.

Functions of the Present Real Conditional
a. To say that something always happens in a specific situation.
b. To talk about a general fact that is always true.
c. To talk about something that may possibly happen in the future (but also may not).
d. To suggest less certainty about the condition.
e. To tell someone to do something (imperative).

_____ **1.** If you want to make a call, please hang up and dial again.

_____ **2.** If you are trying to reach Ms. Landry, she is out of the office on Mondays.

_____ **3.** If you do not press "one" after leaving a message, your message will not be sent.

_____ **4.** If you should need to speak with someone immediately, please call Denise Williamson at extension 4573.

_____ **5.** If you leave a message, Ms. Landry will return your call as soon as possible.

2 Practice

Rewrite the sentences in Practice 1 with the conditional clause at the end of the sentence.

1. _____

2. _____

3. _____

4. _____

5. _____

3 Practice

Give someone advice about visiting your city or country. Use the present real conditional and add the correct punctuation. Write two sentences for each question.

1. What is something that always happens to visitors in your city or country?

   If people visit my (city / country), they _____ .

   People _____ if _____ .

2. What is a general fact about your city or country?

   If _____ , _____ .

   _____ if _____ .

3. What is something that may or may not happen to visitors there?

   If _____ , _____ .

   _____ if _____ .

4. What is a situation that you're not sure about, and what is the possible result?

   If visitors should _____ , they _____ .

   _____ if they should _____ .

5. What is the most important advice you have for visitors? (Use an imperative in the main clause).

   If _____ , _____ .

   _____ if _____ .

14b Unreal Conditional Sentences in the Present or Future

Student Book p. 409

4 Practice

Kimberly is supposed to give a speech in her English class tomorrow. Rewrite the real present conditionals as unreal present conditionals.

1. If Kimberly practices her speech tonight, she won't be nervous tomorrow.

   If Kimberly practiced her speech tonight, she wouldn't be nervous tomorrow.

2. If she delivers a good speech, she will receive a good grade.

   _____

   _____

3. What will happen if she forgets part of her speech?

   _____

4. She can look at her notes if she forgets part of her speech.

   _____

5. She will speak more confidently if she likes the topic.

   _____

6. If Kimberly practices in front of her friends, they can give her feedback.

   _____

7. She will do a better job if she sleeps well tonight.

   _____

8. If her speech is too long or too short, the teacher will lower her grade.

   _____

9. She can practice more if she has the time.

_____

10. If Kimberly is more prepared, she can enjoy giving this speech.

_____

5 Practice

Circle the letter that best describes the meaning of each sentence.

1. If Trisha runs fifty miles a week, she will be ready for the marathon.

   a. This may possibly happen. If she does the weekly running, she will definitely be ready. (a real conditional)

   b. This is a contrary-to-fact or unreal situation. She doesn't run fifty miles a week now. (an unreal conditional)

2. If Trisha won the marathon, she would get $10,000 in prize money.

   a. This may possibly happen. If she wins, she will definitely get $10,000 in prize money. (a real conditional)

   b. This is only a hypothetical situation. (an unreal conditional)

3. She would wear a brace on her knee if it started to hurt.

   a. This may possibly happen. If her knee does hurt, she will wear a brace. (a real conditional)

   b. This is a contrary-to-fact or unreal situation. Her knee doesn't hurt now, and isn't likely to hurt. (an unreal conditional)

4. On the day of the marathon, she would quit running if the weather were too hot.

   a. This may possibly happen. Maybe the weather has already been forecasted to be hot, so if it is really hot, she will quit running. (a real conditional)

   b. This is only a hypothetical situation. This is what she'd do if this were to happen. (an unreal conditional)

5. If Trisha's friends and family come to cheer her on, she'll be very happy.

   a. This may possibly happen. Maybe they live nearby, and if they do come to cheer her on, she will be happy. (a real conditional)

   b. This is an unreal situation. Trisha's friends and family aren't likely to come cheer her on (for whatever reason). (an unreal conditional)

6. While running the marathon, Trisha can stop at a water station if she gets thirsty.

    a. This may possibly happen. Trisha is likely to get thirsty; twenty-six miles is a long way to run! (a real conditional)

    b. This is a contrary-to-fact, hypothetical, or unreal situation. Trisha isn't likely to get thirsty. (an unreal conditional)

7. If she got lost while running the marathon, the race officials would help her to find her way back to the route.

    a. This may possibly happen. Maybe the route is not well-marked. (a real conditional)

    b. This is a contrary-to-fact, hypothetical, or unreal situation. She's not likely to get lost in a major race; the route is well-marked. (an unreal conditional)

8. Trisha couldn't run twenty-six miles if she didn't love running.

    a. This states that something is always true in a specific situation. (a real conditional)

    b. This states a contrary-to-fact condition. Trisha does love running. (an unreal conditional)

6 | Practice

Write what you would or wouldn't do in each situation. Give a reason for your advice.

1. What would you do if you got lost while traveling in a city where you didn't speak the language? Why? _____

_____

_____

_____

2. What would you do if you got a bill that you could not pay? Why?

_____

_____

_____

_____

3. What would you do if you saw someone cheating on a test? Why?

_____

_____

_____

_____

4. What would you do if your house or building caught on fire? Why?

_____

_____

_____

_____

5. What would you do if you were Kimberly (from Practice 4) and you had to give a speech? Why?

_____

_____

_____

_____

14c Unreal Conditional Sentences in the Past; Mixed Conditional Sentences

Student Book p. 412

7 Practice

Read the sentences. Rewrite them as unreal conditional sentences in the past or as mixed conditional sentences. Use the modals in parentheses for the main clause.

1. Raymond learned to ride a bike at an early age. He is such an excellent bicycle messenger today. (would not)

If Raymond hadn't learned to

ride a bike at an early age,

he wouldn't be such an excellent

bicycle messenger today.

2. Raymond's uncle owned a bike messenger company. Raymond got a job there. (might not)

_____

_____

3. Last week, Raymond talked on his cell phone while riding. He got hit by a car. (would not)

_____

_____

4. He was busy talking. He didn't hear the car behind him. (could)

_____

_____

5. He was late meeting a customer. He called to apologize. (would not)

_____

_____

6. The car was going slowly. Therefore, Raymond was not badly injured. (could)

_____

_____

7. Because Raymond's boss is his uncle, Raymond wasn't fired from his job. (might)

_____

_____

8. Raymond isn't afraid to ride his bike in traffic. He returned to work yesterday. (could not)

_____

_____

8 Practice

Reread the sentences you wrote in Practice 7. Write _UP_ if the sentence is an unreal conditional sentence in the past. Write _M_ if the sentence is a mixed conditional.

1. _____   **5.** _____

2. _____   **6.** _____

3. _____   **7.** _____

4. _____   **8.** _____

9 Practice

Complete the sentences with either conditional or main clauses and your own ideas. Use past unreal conditionals or mixed conditionals. Use *might (not), could (not),* or *would (not)* in the main clause.

1. If I hadn't come to this class, _____.

2. _____ if I hadn't studied English.

3. My parents would have been very happy _____.

4. My parents wouldn't have been so happy _____.

5. English would be easier to learn _____.

6. I might not have needed this book _____.

7. _____ if I had paid more attention in class.

8. The teacher would be angry _____.

14d Conditional Sentences with *As If* and *As Though*

Student Book p. 416

10 Practice

Read the sentences. Write *R* next to the sentence if it expresses a real situation. Write *U* if it expresses an unreal situation.

_____ 1. You look as though you're worried about something.

_____ 2. My coworker is acting as if she were the boss.

_____ 3. You talk as if you had already gotten the job.

_____ 4. You talk as though you already have the job.

_____ 5. My boss sounds as if she will leave her position soon.

_____ 6. It seems like my coworker wanted to quit.

11 Practice

Read the sentences. Rewrite the real conditional sentences as unreal, using the simple past or past perfect tense. Rewrite the unreal conditional sentences as real, using the simple present, *be going to,* or *will*. Remember to make changes to the first verb in the sentence as necessary.

1. You look as though you didn't sleep last night.

   You look as though you are tired.

2. It looks as if the sun is going to come out soon.

   _____

3. She talks as if she got the job.

   _____

4. The band sounded like they hadn't practiced.

   _____

5. It looks as though we'll have too much food for the party.

   _____

6. It looks as if there's a big party down the hall.

   _____

7. You look like you know how to solve the problem.

   _____

8. His mother sounded as if she were angry about something.

   _____

12 Practice

Look at the photos. What do you think has happened? What do you think is going to happen? Write two sentences about each photo. Use *as if, as though,* or *like*.

A.

1. *It looks as though the man isn't going to be hurt.*

2. *It looks as if the bicycle tires have slipped in the sand.*

B.

1. _____
   _____
   _____

2. _____
   _____
   _____

C.

1. _____
   _____
   _____
   _____

2. _____
   _____
   _____
   _____

D.

1. _____
   _____
   _____
   _____

2. _____
   _____
   _____
   _____

14e Conditional Sentences Without *If*

Student Book p. 418

13 Practice

Rewrite the sentences in two ways as conditional sentences without *if*. The first time, use inverted subject-verb word order. The second time, use an implied conditional and the words in parentheses.

1. If Matthew had known his parents were coming to visit, he would have cleaned his apartment.

   a. *Had Matthew known his parents were coming to visit,*

   he would have cleaned his apartment.

   b. (otherwise)

   Matthew didn't know his parents were coming to visit.

   Otherwise, he would have cleaned his apartment.

2. If he had had more time, he would have washed the dishes in the sink.

   a. _____

   _____

   b. (with)

   _____

   _____

3. If his mother should see the stains on the rug, she will be upset.

   a. _____

   _____

   b. (might / if so)

   _____

   _____

4. If his friend hadn't helped him, he wouldn't have finished cleaning in time.

   a. _____

   _____

b. (without)

_____

_____

5. If the hotels hadn't been full this weekend, they wouldn't have asked to stay with Matthew.

   a. _____

   _____

   b. (otherwise)

   _____

   _____

6. If Matthew's parents should arrive early, they'll take him out to dinner.

   a. _____

   _____

   b. (might / if so)

   _____

   _____

| 14 | **Practice**

Read the letter of complaint. Rewrite the selected sentences as conditional sentences with _if_.

To the Stimson Luggage Company:

   I am returning a suitcase that I purchased from your company. I have only used it once, on a recent trip to France. <u>Had I known that the suitcase would break so easily</u>, ¹ I never would have bought it. First of all, the handle broke at the airport. <u>Had the handle not broken</u>, ² I wouldn't have had to travel around France with a rope tied to the suitcase.

   In addition to the broken handle, the zipper broke—even though I had only used it five times. It's true that <u>were my suitcase not so full</u>, ³ the zipper might not have broken. However, your company advertises the SuperStrong zipper. Your ad says that <u>should the suitcase get too full</u>, ⁴ the zipper will not break. <u>Had the zipper not broken</u>, ⁵

I wouldn't have lost some of my clothing.

Also, the outside pocket ripped. I didn't realize the fabric was so thin. Otherwise, I
    6
wouldn't have put anything in there.

Were I you, I would carefully test my product before giving false information
    7
about it.

I would like my money refunded. I have enclosed my sales slip. I hope your

company improves its products in the future. If so, I will consider buying another
    8
Stimson suitcase. Until then, however, I will look for another brand.

Sincerely,

Debra Johnson

1. _____

_____

2. _____

_____

3. _____

_____

4. _____

_____

5. _____

_____

6. _____

_____

7. _____

_____

8. _____

_____

14f Wishes About the Present, Future, and Past; *Hope*

Student Book p. 422

15 | Practice

Match the following wishes with the types of wishes.

Types of Wishes
a. Regret about the past
b. A wish for something to change or stop (and that probably won't happen)
c. A wish for something to be different in the present and future
d. A desire for a possible real situation

_____ **1.** I hope I find a job soon. I applied for ten jobs last week!

_____ **2.** I wish I hadn't spent all my money last weekend. Now I don't have any left to go out with my friends this weekend.

_____ **3.** I wish my sister would stop asking to borrow money. I don't have any to give her.

_____ **4.** I can't save money easily. I wish I could save money as well as my brother.

16 | Practice

Luis is trying to do a homework assignment. Write his wishes. You may use or omit *that*. There may be more than one way to rewrite some sentences.

1. Luis doesn't have a computer at home.

    He wishes he had a computer

    at home.

2. He has to use the library computer.

    _____

    _____

3. The Internet connection is slow.

    _____

    _____

4. He can only use the computer for thirty minutes. _____

    _____

5. His friend Joe is telling him jokes. _____

_____

6. He can't print on the library computer. _____

_____

7. He left his floppy disk at home. _____

_____

8. He forgot one of his books. _____

_____

9. He lost his library card. _____

_____

10. He can't finish the assignment. _____

_____

17 Practice

Luis is feeling better about the following situations. Change his negative thoughts to positive thoughts by rewriting the sentences. Rewrite the unreal situations as possible real situations using *hope*. You may use or omit *that*.

1. I don't have enough time to finish the assignment. I wish I had more time.

The library is open for thirty more minutes. *I hope I have enough time to finish the assignment.*

2. The librarian is busy. I wish she could help me.

Now she seems to be free. _____

3. I wish I could buy my own computer. They're so expensive.

I saw a sign in the library. Someone is selling a used computer. _____

_____

4. I wish that my friend had written down the assignment, but he almost never does that.

I saw my friend writing something down in class. _____

_____

5. I wish that people would stop talking. It's so loud!

The librarian just told people to be quiet. _____

_____

6. I wish I had brought money for the photocopy machine. I forgot it.

I hear some change in the bottom of my bag. _____

_____

18 | Practice
Write wishes about your job, school, or class.

1. Write four things you wish were different about your job, school, or class right now.

_____

_____

_____

_____

2. Write four things you wish hadn't happened at your job, school, or class in the past.

_____

_____

_____

_____

3. Write four hopes you have about your job, school, or class.

_____

_____

_____

_____

14g Conditional Sentences with *If Only*

Student Book p. 425

19 Practice

Miguel is looking for a job. Write wishes for him using *if only*. Pay attention to the verb tense.

1. Miguel doesn't have a job right now. He thinks,

   "If only I had a job right now."

2. Miguel doesn't have an MBA. He thinks,

   "_____

   _____."

3. He has to work near his home. He thinks,

   "_____

   _____."

4. He doesn't like to wear suits.

   "_____

   _____."

5. He didn't finish college. "_____."

6. He can't work on weekends. "_____

   _____."

7. He never learned to use a lot of computer programs. "_____

   _____."

8. A job that he wanted was given to someone else. "_____

   _____."

9. He doesn't have a suit to wear to a job interview. "_____

   _____."

10. He didn't start looking for jobs until last week. "_____

_____."

11. He is late paying the rent this month. "_____

_____."

12. He lost his job last month. "_____

_____."

20 Practice

Write six regrets you have about choices you made in the past. Use *if only* and the past perfect.

Examples: *If only I had seen the dentist more often! Then I wouldn't have so many problems with my teeth.*

If only I hadn't taken Route 128! Then I wouldn't have been stuck in traffic for two hours.

_____

_____

_____

_____

_____

_____

_____

_____

_____

_____

_____

SELF-TEST

A Choose the best answer, A, B, C, or D, to complete the sentence. Mark your answer by darkening the oval with the same letter.

1. The movie might not have been so popular if a famous actor _____ in it.

   A. wasn't   Ⓐ Ⓑ Ⓒ Ⓓ
   B. wouldn't have been
   C. isn't
   D. hadn't been

2. It is getting cold outside. It feels _____ it's going to snow.

   A. like if   Ⓐ Ⓑ Ⓒ Ⓓ
   B. as if
   C. though
   D. though if

3. I wish I _____ you with the homework assignment, but I don't understand it.

   A. could help   Ⓐ Ⓑ Ⓒ Ⓓ
   B. should help
   C. would help
   D. would have helped

4. I didn't read that chapter. _____, I would have understood the lecture.

   A. Had I read it   Ⓐ Ⓑ Ⓒ Ⓓ
   B. If I read it
   C. I had read it
   D. If had I read it

5. If you _____ to the supermarket on your way home, please pick up some milk.

   A. went   Ⓐ Ⓑ Ⓒ Ⓓ
   B. will go
   C. would have gone
   D. should go

6. If only I _____ a week, I could have bought that MP3 player on sale.

   A. waited   Ⓐ Ⓑ Ⓒ Ⓓ
   B. had waited
   C. would have waited
   D. would had waited

7. I wouldn't shop there if I _____ you. That store is too expensive.

   A. was   Ⓐ Ⓑ Ⓒ Ⓓ
   B. will be
   C. were
   D. had been

8. Joe is overweight. He wishes that he _____ some weight.

   A. lost   Ⓐ Ⓑ Ⓒ Ⓓ
   B. can lose
   C. could lose
   D. could lost

9. Please give this book to Mary if you _____ her tonight.

   A. see   Ⓐ Ⓑ Ⓒ Ⓓ
   B. would see
   C. had seen
   D. will see

10. Everyone _____ the test if the teacher had given it today.

    A. might had failed   Ⓐ Ⓑ Ⓒ Ⓓ
    B. might have failed
    C. might fail
    D. might failed

B **Find the underlined word or phrase, A, B, C, or D, that is incorrect. Mark your answer by darkening the oval with the same letter.**

1. <u>Before going</u> on a road trip, I
   A

   <u>would check</u> the oil in your car <u>if</u>
   B   **C**

   <u>I am</u> you.
   D

   Ⓐ Ⓑ Ⓒ Ⓓ

2. If you <u>will direct</u> the sunlight <u>to paper</u>
   A   **B**

   with <u>a magnifying glass</u>, the paper
   C

   <u>will burn</u>.
   D

   Ⓐ Ⓑ Ⓒ Ⓓ

3. <u>If only</u> we <u>didn't stay up</u> so late, we
   A   **B**

   <u>wouldn't</u> <u>have missed</u> our morning class.
   C   **D**

   Ⓐ Ⓑ Ⓒ Ⓓ

4. <u>What</u> <u>you will do</u> <u>if</u> you <u>should have</u> a
   A   **B**   **C**   **D**

   problem with your car?

   Ⓐ Ⓑ Ⓒ Ⓓ

5. We <u>were</u> so hungry that <u>we ate</u> <u>like</u> if we
   A   **B**   **C**

   <u>would never see</u> food again.
   D

   Ⓐ Ⓑ Ⓒ Ⓓ

6. Where <u>will</u> <u>you go</u> if you <u>could travel</u>
   A   **B**   **C**

   <u>anywhere in the world</u>?
   D

   Ⓐ Ⓑ Ⓒ Ⓓ

7. Elizabeth doesn't have a car. She <u>wishes</u>
                                      A

   <u>that</u> she <u>doesn't have</u> <u>to take</u> the subway
   B   **C**   **D**

   to work every day.

   Ⓐ Ⓑ Ⓒ Ⓓ

8. If I <u>had been</u> <u>paid</u> today, I <u>could had</u>
   A   **B**   **C**

   <u>bought</u> that new bag.
   D

   Ⓐ Ⓑ Ⓒ Ⓓ

9. I don't like <u>to be</u> around Beth because
   A

   she always <u>sounds</u> <u>though</u> she's <u>having</u> a
   B   **C**   **D**

   bad day.

   Ⓐ Ⓑ Ⓒ Ⓓ

10. My friend <u>might go</u> to college <u>if</u> his high
    A   **B**

    school teachers had <u>encouraged</u> <u>him</u> to.
    C   **D**

    Ⓐ Ⓑ Ⓒ Ⓓ